OECD Public Governance Reviews

Mexico's e-Procurement System

REDESIGNING COMPRANET THROUGH STAKEHOLDER ENGAGEMENT

This document, as well as any data and any map included herein, are without prejudice to the status of or sovereignty over any territory, to the delimitation of international frontiers and boundaries and to the name of any territory, city or area.

Please cite this publication as:
OECD (2018), *Mexico's e-Procurement System: Redesigning CompraNet through Stakeholder Engagement*, OECD Public Governance Reviews, OECD Publishing, Paris.
http://dx.doi.org/10.1787/9789264287426-en

ISBN 978-92-64-28741-9 (print)
ISBN 978-92-64-28742-6 (PDF)

Series: OECD Public Governance Reviews
ISSN 2219-0406 (print)
ISSN 2219-0414 (online)

Photo credits: Cover ©vs148/shutterstock.com; ©Till Teenck/Thenounproject.com; ©Adrien Coquet/thenounproject.com; ©Garagestock/Shutterstock.com; ©Faisalovers/thenounproject.com; ©Iconsphere/thenounproject.com.

Corrigenda to OECD publications may be found on line at: *www.oecd.org/about/publishing/corrigenda.htm*.
© OECD 2018

You can copy, download or print OECD content for your own use, and you can include excerpts from OECD publications, databases and multimedia products in your own documents, presentations, blogs, websites and teaching materials, provided that suitable acknowledgement of OECD as source and copyright owner is given. All requests for public or commercial use and translation rights should be submitted to *rights@oecd.org*. Requests for permission to photocopy portions of this material for public or commercial use shall be addressed directly to the Copyright Clearance Center (CCC) at *info@copyright.com* or the Centre français d'exploitation du droit de copie (CFC) at *contact@cfcopies.com*.

Foreword

Public procurement is a key economic activity for governments and how it is carried out has a major impact on how taxpayers' money is used to deliver public services. In Mexico, expenditure on public procurement is equal to roughly USD 111.5 billion per year, accounting for 21% of the government's expenditure in 2015. As the public sector is a critical driver of productivity in the economy, the impact of public expenditure on the national interest goes beyond delivering public services. Governments generate productivity through the amount they spend, but also by developing and supporting the environment that creates the right conditions for firms to invest and innovate, and for societies to thrive.

The efficiency and integrity of Mexico's public services, in particular in relation to the use of public funds, is subject to scrutiny by a variety of stakeholders. The cross-cutting nature of public procurement, and its vulnerability to acts of corruption, has rightly brought attention to the need to ensure public funds are spent effectively and fairly. The continuing efforts by the federal government to increase efficiency in public spending and minimise the risk of corruption have been undermined by missteps that damage public perception of government procurement. Eliminating corruption is an important part of the effort to increase productivity as it affects the key determinants of productivity growth, which are innovation and diffusion of new technologies, an enabling market environment, and resource allocation. Therefore, mitigating corruption risk is a significant step on a country's path towards sustainable and inclusive development.

The peer review, *'Mexico's e-Procurement System: Redesigning CompraNet Through Stakeholder Engagement'* highlights that changes to the procurement system are needed not only to show that the use of public funds in providing public services is both effective and fair, but also to rebuild public trust. The digitalisation of government activity presents an opportunity to radically improve government's interaction with citizens, businesses and civil society. In this respect, the OECD's Recommendation of the Council on Digital Government Strategies supports policies and approaches that achieve greater transparency, openness and inclusiveness of government processes and operations. Experiences from OECD countries have demonstrated how e-procurement has the potential to achieve these goals.

Since 1996, the federal government has used the CompraNet system to engage with the supply market. At its inception, CompraNet was a ground-breaking approach to e-procurement in Latin America. It is a critical interface for government and suppliers alike, and has been a powerful tool for increasing the participation of small and medium-sized businesses (SMEs) in government contracting. The current administration now wishes to take advantage of developments in technology to identify a vision for the future of the system. Current trends indicate that the next generation of e-procurement reform will involve digital integration across government agencies, but also linking to other government systems, such as finance and tax. This will enable data to be collected and used to ensure the accountability of government spending in the short-term, and importantly, to shape government policy in the long-term.

The OECD was invited by the Ministry of Public Administration (*Secretaría de la Función Pública*, SFP) to bring together the perspectives of a broad range of stakeholders into a single vision that aligns with global best practices. If implemented effectively, the reform of CompraNet will lift civil service productivity, improve the quality and reduce the cost of goods and services bought by government. It will also be a milestone in the rollout of the National Digital Strategy, which will serve as a catalyst for the country's growth under the National Development Plan.

The roadmap presented in this peer review outlines a phased approach for re-designing the system. This approach enables close monitoring of delivery and, in a country where e-procurement is well entrenched, eases the impact of change on all users. The first phase of the roadmap will seek to mitigate some of the greatest integrity risks by improving system compliance. The second phase, a stepping-stone toward system integration, would allow procurement information to be collected and re-purposed in open data format. This will support the third and last phase, an eventual transition to a fully transactional system that is integrated with other government systems.

The evolution of CompraNet through these three phases is expected to bring about incremental improvements in the system's efficiency and effectiveness. Given CompraNet's broad reach across economic activity in Mexico, the spillover effects of these improvements can result in increases in the productivity of government employees, the digital capabilities and competitiveness of suppliers, value for money from government spending, and public trust in government institutions.

Angel Gurría
OECD Secretary-General

Acknowledgements

Under the direction and oversight of the Director for Public Governance, and János Bertók, Head of the Public Sector Integrity Division, this review was co-ordinated by Jacobo Pastor García Villarreal, Senior Policy Analyst, with the support of Paulo Magina, Head of the OECD Public Procurement Unit. The authors of the report were Andy Cochrane and Juan Pablo Bolaños.

Valuable comments and suggestions were received from Matthieu Cahen. Editorial assistance was provided by Thibaut Gigou, Meral Gedik and Victoria Elliott. Pauline Alexandrov, Alpha Zambou, Edwina Collins and Nadjad Bacar provided administrative assistance.

The OECD expresses its gratitude to Mexico's Ministry of Public Administration (SFP) for its co-operation and leadership, in particular to Minister Arely Gómez González; Deputy Minister for Public Administration, Eber Betanzos Torres; Deputy Minister for Administrative Responsibilities and Public Procurement, José Gabriel Carreño Camacho; Head of the Unit for Public Procurement Policy, Alejandro Luna; Head of the Open Government and International Co-operation Policies, Alejandra Rascón; and the entire team and all the departments of the SFP and Mexico's government involved in this process. Ambassador Mónica Aspe and Maya Alejandra Camacho Dávalos, of the Permanent Delegation of Mexico to the OECD, helped support the OECD in this project.

This review is part of a series of peer reviews on public procurement in OECD, G20 and non-member economies. It benefited from input from senior public procurement officials who participated in the OECD Meeting of the Working Party of Leading Practitioners on Public Procurement held in Paris on 16-18 October 2017, chaired by Dag Stromsnes, Chief Procurement Officer, Agency for Public Management and e-Government (Difi) in Norway. Special thanks go to the lead reviewers: María Margarita Zuleta, until recently the Director General of *Colombia Compra Eficiente*, and Guillermo Burr Ortúzar, Head of Research and Business Intelligence, *Chile Compra*.

This review also benefited from input from senior officials of the Superior Audit Body (ASF), the Economic Competition Federal Commission (COFECE), the National Institute on Transparency, Freedom of Information and Personal Data Protection (INAI), and the Executive Secretariat to the National Anti-corruption System, as well as from civil society organisations and chambers of commerce participating in the Plural Working Group on Public Procurement.

The OECD Mexico Centre, under the leadership of Roberto Martinez, and its publications staff, notably Alejandro Camacho, co-ordinated the editorial process for the Spanish publication.

The review was approved by the OECD Working Party of the Leading Practitioners on Public Procurement (LPP) on 27 November 2017 and declassified by the Public Governance Committee on 21 December 2017.

Table of contents

Foreword 3

Acknowledgements 5

Abbreviations and Acronyms 10

Executive summary 13
    Key recommendations 14

Chapter 1. A multi-stakeholder review of the effectiveness of Mexico's CompraNet system 15
    Reforms have improved CompraNet, but it must continue to evolve 16
    SFP convened stakeholders in a well-defined, co-ordinated governance structure 25
    Note 35
    References 36

Chapter 2. Upgrading CompraNet to a system that delivers for all stakeholders 37
    Reinforcing CompraNet's role in enabling public procurement reform 38
    A user-friendly system providing easily accessible, open and reliable data 50
    Using CompraNet to improve procurement practices, encourage competition and optimise value for public money 60
    Note 70
    References 71

Chapter 3. A multi-phase roadmap for upgrading CompraNet from compliance to integration 73
    A comprehensive programme for the CompraNet Roadmap 74
    References 82

Annex A. System 'Vision' 83

Annex B. Subgroup recommendations 85

Tables

Table 1.1. Subgroup themes and objectives 28
Table 2.1. Data needs of typical stakeholders 57
Table 2.2. Techniques for managing data integrity issues 59
Table 2.3. Average monthly help desk Statistics at *Colombia Compra Eficiente* (2017) 61
Table 3.1. Roadmap actions 79

Table A A.1. Timetable for developing a vision statement for Mexico's e-Procurement System 84
Table A B.1. Information quality ranking 86
Table A B.2. Information-gathering methods, by Subgroup 87

Table A B.3. Single Formats for Observations and Recommendations, by sub group 88
Table A B.4. Aggregated recommendations 89
Table A B.5. Timetable for developing Subgroup recommendations on CompraNet 89

Figures

Figure 1.1. Information flows and limitations of the current CompraNet system 21
Figure 1.2. Integrity risks and efficiencies in the procurement process, and e-procurement
    mitigations 24
Figure 1.3. Organisation chart for the Plural Working Group on Public Procurement 26
Figure 1.4. Summary of Plenary Meetings from February to November 2017 29
Figure 2.1. Challenges facing contracting authorities in OECD countries in using e-procurement 40
Figure 2.2. Facets of an e-procurement Strategy 41
Figure 2.3. Illustration of the evolution of technology in procurement over time 43
Figure 2.4. Comparison of the scope of CompraNet vs. contracting authorities' systems 44
Figure 2.5. Functionalities of e-procurement systems in OECD countries 45
Figure 2.6. Horizontal versus vertical integration 46
Figure 2.7. Challenges for businesses in effectively using e-procurement systems 64
Figure 2.8. Approaches in place in OECD countries supporting the development of SMEs 66
Figure 3.1. Procurement levers by level of flexibility 75
Figure 3.2. CompraNet Roadmap 77

Boxes

Box 1.1. Mexican legislation on public procurement and CompraNet 18
Box 1.2. OECD's Recommendation of the Council on Public Procurement – Principle on
    e-procurement 23
Box 1.3. OECD's Recommendation of the Council on Public Procurement – principle
    on participation 27
Box 1.4. Methods for the collection and analysis of information 30
Box 1.5. IT Development Programme 1995-2000 31
Box 1.6. Vision for Mexico's federal government e-procurement system 33
Box 2.1. A comprehensive e-procurement strategy in Slovakia 42
Box 2.2. The integrated e-procurement system KONEPS in Korea 47
Box 2.3. Korea's system integration has cut the cost of procurement transactions 48
Box 2.4. Horizontal system integration with national finance in Colombia 50
Box 2.5. OECD's Recommendation of the Council on Public Procurement – principle on
    transparency 51
Box 2.6. Linking systems of accountability and transparency: *Subsidios al Campo* in Mexico 52
Box 2.7. Open Contracting Data Standard in Ukraine 54
Box 2.8. Korea's Bid-Rigging Indicator Analysis System (BRIAS) 56
Box 2.9. Stakeholder training and e-procurement support in Colombia 62
Box 2.10. OECD's Recommendation of the Council on Public Procurement – principle on capacity . 63
Box 2.11. OECD's Recommendation of the Council on Public Procurement – principle on access 65
Box 2.12. A whistle-blower hotline in Austria 67
Box 2.13. Government Model Contracts in New Zealand 69

Follow OECD Publications on:

http://twitter.com/OECD_Pubs

http://www.facebook.com/OECDPublications

http://www.linkedin.com/groups/OECD-Publications-4645871

http://www.youtube.com/oecdilibrary

http://www.oecd.org/oecddirect/

Abbreviations and Acronyms

ADB	Asian Development Bank
ASF	Superior Audit Body (Auditoría Superior de la Federación)
BI	Business Intelligence
BRIAS	Korea's Bid-Rigging Indicator Analysis System
CCE	Consejo Coordinador Empresarial
COFECE	Economic Competition Federal Commission (Comisión Federal de Competencia Económica)
CPB	Central Purchasing Body
CPO	Chief Procurement Officer
CSO	Civil Society Organisation
CUCOP	Mexico's procurement cataloguing system (Clasificador Único de las Contrataciones Públicas)
DOF	Official Journal of the Federation (Diario Oficial de la Federación)
EUR	Euro
FTC	Fair Trade Commission in Korea
GDP	Gross Domestic Product
GMC	Government Model Contract (in New Zealand)
ICT	Information and Communications Technology
IMCO	Mexican Institute for Competitiveness (Instituto Mexicano para la Competitividad)
IMSS	Mexico's Social Security Institute (Instituto Mexicano del Seguro Social)
INAI	National Institute on Transparency, Freedom of Information and Personal Data Protection (Instituto Nacional de Transparencia, Acceso a la Información y Protección de Datos Personales)
INADEM	National Institute for Entrepreneurs (Instituto Nacional del Emprendedor)
IT	Information and Technology
LAASSP	Law on Public Sector Acquisitions, Leases and Services (Ley de Adquisiciones, Arrendamientos y Servicios del Sector Público)

LOPSRM	Law on Public Works and Related Services (Ley de Obras Públicas y Servicios Relacionados con las Mismas)
KONEPS	Korea's e-Procurement system
KRW	Korean won
OCDS	Open Contracting Data Standard
OCP	Open Contracting Partnership (Alianza para las contrataciones abiertas)
OECD	Organisation for Economic Co-operation and Development
MBIE	Ministry of Business, Innovation and Employment in New Zealand
MCCI	Mexicans Against Corruption and Impunity (Mexicanos Contra la Corrupción y la Impunidad)
MXN	Mexican peso
RIA	Regulatory Impact Analysis
RUPC	Supplier Registry (Registro Único de Proveedores y Contratistas)
PPS	Public Procurement Services in Korea
PwC	PricewaterhouseCoopers
SAT	Tax Revenue Agency (Sistema de Administración Tributaria)
SaaS	Software as a Service
SECODAM	Ministry of the Comptrollership and Administrative Development (Secretaría de la Contraloría y Desarrollo Administrativo, 1994-2000)
SECOP II	Electronic System for Public Contracts (Sistema Electrónico para la Contratación Pública)
SFP	Ministry of Public Administration (Secretaría de la Función Pública)
SGC	Subgroup Co-ordinator
SICOP	Accountability and Budget System (Sistema de Contabilidad y Presupuesto)
SIDEC	SFP's complaint system (Sistema Integral de Denuncias Ciudadanas)
SIIP	Integrated System of Financial Information (Sistema Integrado de Información Financiera)
SME	Small and Medium-size Enterprise
TS	Technical Secretariat
UNCITRAL	United Nations Commission on International Trade Law
UNSPC	United Nations Standard Products and Services Code
UNWRA	United Nations Relief and Works Agency
UPAGCI	Unit of Open Government and International Co-operation Policies (Unidad de Políticas de Apertura Gubernamental y Cooperación Internacional)

UPCP	Unit for Public Procurement Policy (Unidad de Política de Contrataciones Públicas)
USD	United States dollar
VS	Vision Statement
WKStA	Public Prosecutor's Office against Corruption and White-Collar Crime in Germany (Zentrale Staatsanwaltschaft zur Verfolgung von Wirtschaftsstrafsachen und Korruption)

Executive summary

Taxpayers increasingly demand trustworthy and efficient public spending, particularly at times of fiscal consolidation. Governments in OECD countries are paying greater attention to the way they spend scarce budgetary resources, and Mexico is no exception. Restoring trust in public institutions has been central to many recent reforms and initiatives by Mexico's government. The sheer size of public procurement and its heightened exposure to risk provide clear opportunities to restore public confidence not only in the integrity of the government, but also in its efficiency.

In addition to laws and regulations, the evolution of the technology used in procurement generates a spillover effect on the entire system, since it can radically change the way in which procurement operations are conducted and reported. E-procurement platforms have long been used by OECD countries to promote transparency, and CompraNet has always been seen as a crucial tool in that endeavour. Recent advances in technology now provide public authorities with new possibilities for improving efficiency and strategic risk management in procurement.

The OECD report *Mexico's E-procurement System: Redesigning CompraNet through Stakeholder Engagement* provides an assessment of the current scope of the system, how it operates, and how well it is suited to supporting efficient, effective and transparent public procurement in Mexico. Reforming CompraNet will entail upgrading the system, so that in addition to allowing access to government procurement documents, it can offer a more strategic approach to procurement. This will help identify weaknesses in the procurement cycle where technology can help streamline the process and minimise exposure to risk.

Introducing e-procurement reform will involve a multitude of stakeholders with different and sometimes conflicting interests. Stakeholder engagement has so far been broad and comprehensive, resulting in an inclusive and collaborative reform process led by the Ministry of Public Administration (*Secretaría de la Función Pública*, SFP). Leading figures in business, civil society and the public sector were invited to help develop recommendations to enhance CompraNet, and a Plural Working Group on Public Procurement was established. The objective of the Working Group was to build consensus on upgrading and expanding the CompraNet system.

To achieve the desired results, SFP will need to focus on implementation. A phased approach will enable closer monitoring and control of delivery, while reducing the impact of change on system users and other stakeholders. A roadmap for CompraNet has been developed, taking into account the specific context of Mexico and the current state of the CompraNet system. Three phases (for the short, medium and long term) were distinguished, so that CompraNet can evolve from a compliance-driven system into a platform that generates procurement intelligence and, in the third phase, a fully integrated transactional system.

Key recommendations

Align the e-procurement strategy with a broad and co-ordinated reform programme.

The e-procurement system should be part of a multifaceted programme that aligns with other aspects of procurement reform (such as legal and policy settings, or the private sector environment). If considerable changes to CompraNet are seen simply as a technology enhancement project, without an accompanying reform of procurement, the project may not achieve the anticipated benefits.

Work towards a more efficient, effective and transparent e-procurement process.

The focus for e-procurement systems in OECD countries has recently shifted from a platform for transparency and disclosure of public procurement opportunities towards helping to increase efficiency and effectiveness in public procurement. This requires identifying the stages of the procurement cycle where technological solutions are most needed.

Ensure integrity in public procurement processes.

Despite efforts to provide an institutional, legal and regulatory framework to prevent corruption in public procurement, citizens' trust in government institutions and activities remains low, and the perception of corruption is still high. SFP and Mexico's Federal Government could benefit from building a coherent and efficient institutional and normative public procurement framework, including dedicated measures intended to combat corruption and better manage public funds. A system like CompraNet can contribute by minimising direct contact between public procurement officials and bidders and by establishing electronic records of procurement operations for the purposes of audit and oversight.

Public procurement officials should be trained in the skills needed for e-procurement tools.

In addition to implementing recommendations related to technical changes and process improvements, SFP should also identify ways to overcome other barriers to the effective functioning of the public procurement process. Procurement practitioners require additional support and guidance to carry out their roles effectively. The data gathered during the OECD's mission suggest that the low number of enquiries to CompraNet's help desk reflects a lack of familiarity with the system's processes and norms.

Robust open data practices can standardise public procurement data and enhance accountability mechanisms.

A large amount of information on Mexico's public procurement activity is available in CompraNet, but it is not comprehensive, and it is not available in formats that can help to increase accountability. The quality of insights that can be extracted from the system will affect its ability to increase accountability, guide public policy design and generate value for public funds. Public disclosure of high-quality data is necessary, in a format that allows for analysis of trends and exceptions. CompraNet should thus aim to provide shareable, reusable and machine-readable data that make it possible to develop statistics and conduct data analysis.

Chapter 1. A multi-stakeholder review of the effectiveness of Mexico's CompraNet system

By gaining the input and perspective of key stakeholders, the project to reform the Mexican e-procurement system has benefited from the broad experience of contracting authorities, supplier groups and civil society. The CompraNet system has gradually developed into an effective tool to facilitate the federal government's engagement with the private sector. However, this third-generation reform presents an opportunity to develop a long-term vision for the system, and to ensure that future developments are in line with global trends. This chapter provides the context for the reform project, and describes how the engagement approach has been designed to ensure that the system upgrade will address stakeholders' concerns.

The CompraNet system has evolved since its inception in 1996 along with governmental reforms to increase the efficiency, effectiveness and accountability of public institutions. Developments to the system have enabled the Mexican federal government to streamline public procurement activities and make them more transparent. The objectives of the system, which this chapter covers in greater detail, are to increase the efficiency and transparency of public procurement. Feedback from stakeholders, and comparison with international best practice, suggest that these aspects of the system can be further improved.

SFP commissioned this review to identify how CompraNet can be upgraded to help overcome the system's current challenges, and to outline a vision for the future that aligns with current trends in e-procurement. SFP sought to develop an inclusive process to gather stakeholder perspectives on the weaknesses of the current system and a vision for the future. Engagement with stakeholders throughout the project has been broad and comprehensive, and provides a benchmark for other countries wishing to undertake e-procurement reforms in an inclusive, collaborative fashion.

To generate broad consensus for the third generation of CompraNet reforms, SFP decided to invite stakeholders to form a working group supported by several subgroups focused on different thematic streams. The Subgroups of the Plural Working Group on Public Procurement (the "Subgroups"), featuring representatives of key organisations, such as internal auditors, contracting authorities, suppliers and civil society, reached out to their networks through surveys and interviews, to ensure that the opinions of those that they represented were reflected in the process. This was brought together through a co-ordinated and transparent governance structure with high-level project ownership. Working Group meetings were led by the Minister for Public Administration, and included deputy ministers and senior officials. These meetings monitored progress against key project milestones and helped determine the goals of the project and to develop a consensus-based Vision Statement for the system. Based on these solid foundations, the strategy for the system has now been formulated both to meet stakeholders' needs and to reflect international best practice.

The vision for CompraNet, drafted by stakeholders and co-ordinated by SFP and the OECD, aims to overcome the system's challenges by aligning the system with global best practice. The statement outlines the kind of outcomes that can be expected of a well-functioning public procurement environment and an efficient, effective e-procurement system.

Reforms have improved CompraNet, but it must continue to evolve

CompraNet has improved over time to meet government goals of increasing efficiency and integrity

Legislative and political context

Within the framework of the "Good Governance Agenda" established in 1982 (Dussauge, 2010[1]), Mexico's federal government has embarked on a series of reforms to make public administration more efficient and effective. Policies of auditing, transparency, regulatory improvement, anti-corruption and the introduction of management practices in the day-to-day administration of public organisations have been instituted. The Ministry of the General Comptroller (*Secretaría de la Contraloría General de la Federación*), created during the 1982-1988 presidential term to enhance the system of accountability for the federal public administration, was replaced by the Ministry of the Comptrollership and Administrative Development (*Secretaría de la Contraloría y Desarrollo Administrativo,* SECODAM) in the 1994-2000 administration. This change of name reflected the extension of its responsibilities, and the intent to modernise the government's administrative function. The first three versions of CompraNet were developed under the leadership of SECODAM. In the 2000-2006 administration, the ministry's name was changed again to the Ministry of Public Administration (*Secretaría de la Función Pública,* SFP), whose new responsibilities included programmes to increase professionalisation in the civil service (Pardo, 2009[2]).

Starting in 2015, Mexico's federal government instituted a series of reforms to strengthen its public integrity system, including reinforcing integrity standards for public procurement officials. In early 2015, a series of executive orders were issued by the president. The eight actions focused on preventing and managing conflicts of interest and integrity risks. They also included four initiatives on the management of public procurement processes:

- **A protocol of conduct for public servants in public procurement**, and on granting and extension of licenses, permits, authorisations and concessions (*Acuerdo por el que se expide el protocolo de actuación en materia de contrataciones públicas, otorgamiento y prórroga de licencias, permisos, autorizaciones y concesiones*). This is part of the General Law on Administrative Responsibilities (*Ley General de Responsabilidades Administrativas*).
- **A registry of federal administration public servants involved in procurement processes** (*Registro de servidores públicos de la Administración Pública Federal que intervienen en procedimientos de contrataciones públicas*), including classification by their level of responsibility and their certification.
- **An online list of sanctioned suppliers**, specifying the reason for the sanction.
- **Increased collaboration with the private sector** to reinforce transparency in procurement procedures and decision making. It also aims to increase integrity by asking citizens to help identify vulnerable processes, as well as developing co-operation agreements with chambers of commerce and civil society organisations.

These developments coincided with the introduction of CompraNet as the government's e-procurement platform and the designation of SFP as the public body entrusted with developing and managing the system. In 2009, the reforms to the Law on Public Sector Acquisitions, Leases and Services (LAASSP) and the Law on Public Works and Related Services (LOPSRM) gave CompraNet legal status as the official platform for managing electronic information on the federal government's procurement activity. Government entities subject to this legislation were required to use CompraNet in the procurement procedures prescribed under both laws.

Reform proposals for the laws regulating acquisitions of goods, services and public works were recently presented in Congress. These efforts should consider the recommendations of this review, such as system interoperability, to ensure that the legal and system changes are fully compatible. These proposals are currently being analysed, and formal amendments may be introduced into the legislative agenda. This review, including the collaborative work of the Plural Working Group on Public Procurement, is expected to inform the process of implementing the recommendations made for CompraNet and to be carried forward by subsequent administrations, given that the work done so far represents the common vision of major stakeholders involved in public procurement.

Box 1.1. Mexican legislation on public procurement and CompraNet

The legal and regulatory framework for public procurement in Mexico allows for e-procurement to assist government in conducting procurement processes and awarding contracts electronically. The core legislative requirements for e-procurement and e-commerce deal with electronic documents and electronic signatures, but the law touches on different facets of public procurement in a number of ways. At the federal level, the applicable legal provisions in public procurement address the following areas:

- three laws governing procurement and public works
- a number of secondary regulations and administrative instruments
- obligations arising from international agreements.

This legal framework is broad and complex, and is complicated by the number of laws relating to procurement at the state level. The current procurement legislation is now under review, to help identify improvements that could make public procurement operate more effectively. A representative from the Anti-Corruption Commission of the Senate attended the fifth Plenary Meeting to extend this discussion. It should be noted that passing and then implementing any new laws is likely to be a lengthy process involving the efforts of many stakeholders. Many countries regulate procurement practices using a number of other instruments, for example through policies, directives and training, as well as through the functionality of the e-procurement system itself.

Source: Revision of current legislation; (Asian Development Bank, 2013[3]).

Technical context

Since it was launched in 1996, CompraNet has been expanded and new modules have been added. The tool has evolved from a platform for publicising tender opportunities and disclosing contract award decisions into a portal where government agencies can post tender documents (CompraNet 5.0, launched in 2010). Incremental changes and improvements have been introduced in response to technological developments and government needs.

The first three versions of the tool were developed by SFP's predecessor, SECODAM (1994-2000), as part of a pilot project that produced CompraNet 1.0 (1996), CompraNet 2.0 (1997), and CompraNet 3.0 (2000). The most significant features of each version were as follows:

- 1.0: module to publicise tender opportunities and disclose contract award decisions
- 2.0: access to bidding opportunity documents, upon receipt of a bank slip to prove payment of fees related to federal legal rights
- 3.0: a transaction module to allow for e-tendering.

The first two versions of the system allowed suppliers to search for current government tender opportunities and obtain copies of bidding documents, upon receipt of a bank slip, as proof of payment of fees related to federal legal rights. This lowered transaction costs for suppliers, as historically suppliers had to collect bidding documents from public buying units. CompraNet version 3.0 was adopted after the publication of a Secretariat Agreement in the Official Gazette on 9 August 2000. From that date on, different federal entities and agencies gradually introduced the system for their own procurement processes. Version 3.0 allowed for electronic submission of bid documents and contract award notices.

CompraNet Plus (4.0) was launched in 2007, but ran into performance issues. After six months, the pilot implementation project was canceled, and Version 4.0 never replaced CompraNet 3.0. Nevertheless, during OECD's fact-finding mission, several users indicated that they believed this version was the most user-friendly to date.

CompraNet 5.0 was launched in 2010. Its current scope of activity originates from a web-based platform developed by Bravo Solutions, which was identified as a system able to enact Mexican procurement legislation. The system would enable:

- buyers, private businesses and interested stakeholders to register, even remotely, to gain access to government tender documents
- uploading of documentation related to non-open tender activity, such as closed tenders (invitations to three businesses) and direct awards, both permissible by law under certain circumstances
- loading and sharing of the annual procurement plans developed by government agencies
- execution of various forms of e-auction, including English/reverse and Dutch auctions
- traceability of user activities, such as loading and accessing of documentation
- online training for buyers
- extraction and analysis of data from the Datamart database
- development of a supplier registry, against which government buyers can provide ratings (on a 0-100 scale) to record contract compliance
- execution of tender activities, including the dissemination of documentation such as minutes of clarification meetings, testimonies of social witnesses, executed contracts and any variations or modifications.

Additional enhancements were introduced in 2015, including a new "comprehensive technical support" scheme which aimed to achieve 99.5% availability for CompraNet users, as well as additional security for the Datamart. Another field, the *Clave Cartera*, was added to procurement activities. This relates to investment programmes and projects, and opens the door to linkages being developed between procurement activities and the Ministry of Finance's information on public grants and funding.

This is reflected in the main objectives of the CompraNet system, as described in Mexican federal legislation and the corresponding manuals of operation, which are intended to:

- help develop a general policy on procurement processes
- facilitate transparency and follow up on procurement processes
- generate adequate information for planning and budgeting
- improve procurement process efficiency to guarantee quality in public services.

Systemic changes in public procurement could rebuild trust in the integrity of public spending

The goals listed above concern the importance of CompraNet's role in increasing the efficiency and effectiveness of public procurement processes, providing stakeholders enough information to develop procurement policies to conduct "follow-up to procurement processes" where necessary and to undertake planning and budgeting. CompraNet has encountered some challenges in carrying out this mandate. The diagram below shows how the current operation of the system and its application by users fall short of these objectives.

Figure 1.1. Information flows and limitations of the current CompraNet system

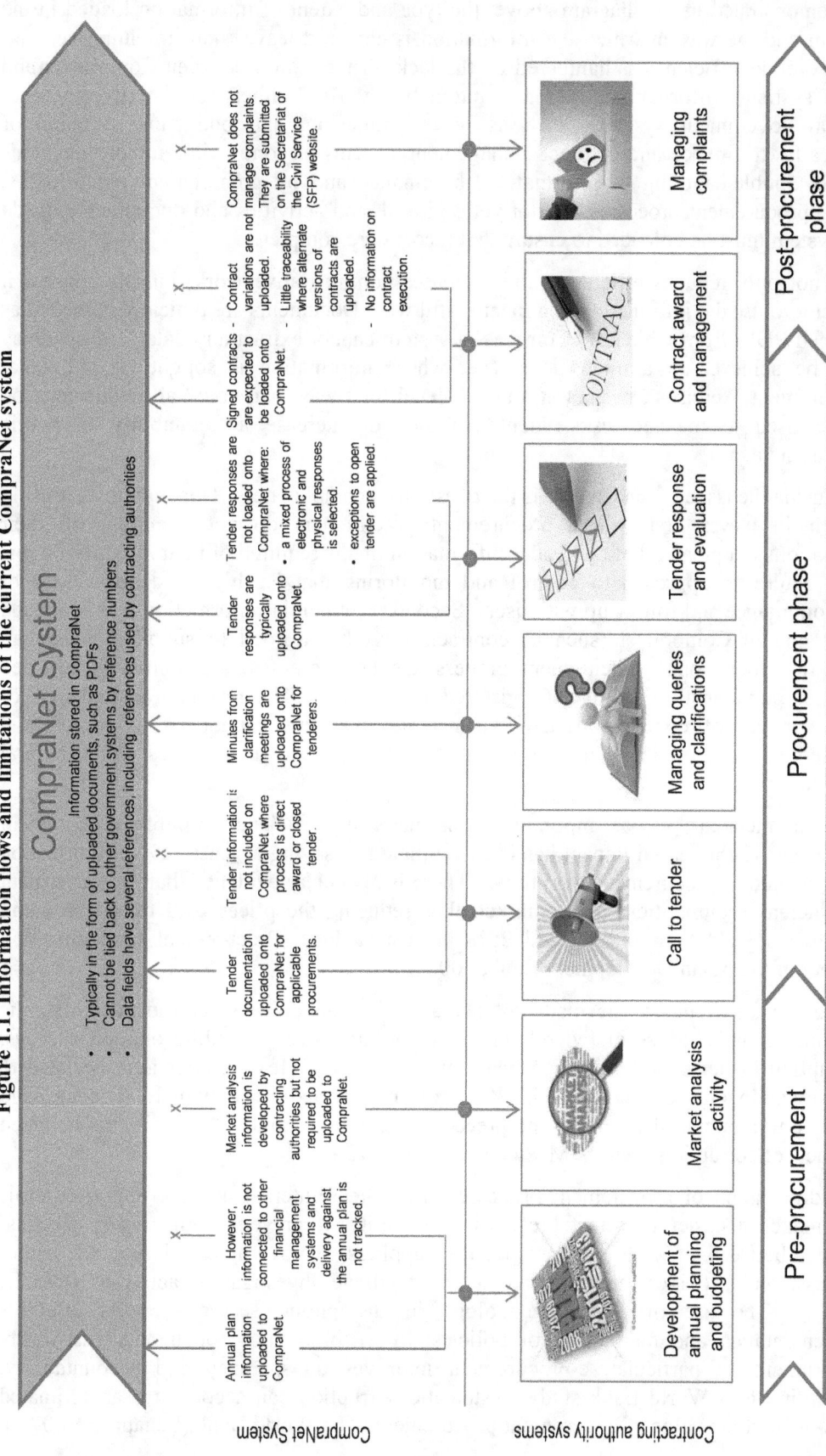

Source: Courtesy of system information provided by SFP.

As demonstrated in the diagram above, the type and extent of information loaded in the system and the way in which the information is captured leave room for improvement. For example, efficiency is hampered by the lack of integration between CompraNet and other systems. Information does not automatically flow either horizontally (to other central government systems, such as federal financing and budgeting systems) or vertically (to finance and contract management systems of contracting authorities). This entails double-handling of information; by finance and by procurement practitioners. Many procurement processes are not yet digitised, and activities and documents outside the system must be uploaded to ensure that records are complete.

This not only reduces efficiency and increases administrative work, but also makes it difficult to use the information in a meaningful way. Documents are typically uploaded as scanned PDFs from which the CompraNet system cannot extract any data. Transparency may be achieved at a micro level (i.e. where information is sought on individual procurement exercises), but not at a macro-level, in a way that would allow information to be used to manage risks, identify trends or increase accountability in public procurement.

Alongside the issue of data access is the question of completeness. This manifests itself in two main ways; first, where procurement practitioners do not comply with their obligations to upload all of the tender information that is required of them. Rectifying this will require an approach to control and monitoring that is able to identify cases of noncompliance and follow up with users. Second, commercial information that is outside the scope of CompraNet (such as contracts directly awarded to suppliers where an exception to an open procurement process has been granted, and contracts awarded between public institutions) is not registered in the system. This results in a blind spot for the oversight of commercial activity, meaning that this cannot be monitored and stakeholders cannot obtain a complete picture of commercial activities at the federal level.

E-procurement can play an important role in increasing efficiency in public procurement processes. The potential impact has been estimated as saving at least 12% in transaction costs related to procurement workflows. There is also clear evidence that e-procurement can increase competition in the market, thus reducing the prices paid by government, which can yield between 5% and 25% in cost savings (Procurement Harmonization Project of the Asian Development Bank, 2004[4]).

There are also gains to be made to increase Mexican citizens' confidence in public institutions and the use of federal funds. According to recent public opinion surveys, corruption is the second most significant problem facing Mexico, after issues related to security and violence. As of 2015, 27% of citizens reported that they had paid some kind of bribe to a public official over the preceding 12 months, and 92% of citizens believed that acts of corruption occur in Mexico (Marván, 2015[5]).

The digitisation of procurement processes strengthens internal anti-corruption controls and makes it easier to detect breaches of integrity. It prevents unnecessary physical contact between officials and prospective suppliers to government during the tender process, and provides audit trails that can facilitate investigation activities (OECD, 2016[6]). The use of digital technology in the public sector supports effective implementation and monitoring of policies, by enabling more open and trustworthy government. In particular, e-procurement improves transparency and accountability. According to a World Bank study, systematic corruption can account for an estimated 20%-30% of the value of government procurement (The World Bank; Schapper, 2007[7]).

These benefits have long been understood and appreciated by member countries, which helps explain why all OECD countries surveyed have implemented e-procurement systems (OECD, 2016[8]).

> **Box 1.2. OECD's Recommendation of the Council on Public Procurement – Principle on e-procurement**
>
> VII. RECOMMENDS that Adherents improve the public procurement system by harnessing the use of digital technologies to support appropriate e-procurement innovations throughout the procurement cycle.
>
> To this end, Adherents should:
>
> i) Employ recent digital technology developments that allow **integrated e-procurement solutions** covering the procurement cycle. Information and communication technologies should be used in public procurement to ensure transparency and access to public tenders, **increasing competition, simplifying processes** for contract award and management, driving cost savings and **integrating public procurement and public finance information**.
>
> ii) Pursue state-of-the-art e-procurement tools that are modular, flexible, scalable and secure, in order to assure business continuity, privacy and integrity, provide fair treatment and protect sensitive data, while supplying the core capabilities and functions that allow business innovation. E-procurement tools should be **simple to use and appropriate to their purpose**, and consistent across procurement agencies, to the extent possible; excessively complicated systems could create implementation risks and challenges for new entrants or small and medium enterprises.
>
> *Source:* (OECD, 2015[9]).

As illustrated in the diagram below, risks posed to integrity can emerge at many different phases of the procurement cycle and in different ways. Similarly, process inefficiencies occur at each phase of the procurement process. To mitigate the risks and increase process efficiencies requires a comprehensive, well-co-ordinated reform programme, with e-procurement as a critical tool in a broader effort.

Figure 1.2. Integrity risks and efficiencies in the procurement process, and e-procurement mitigations

Phase	Step	Integrity risks	Inefficiencies	E-procurement mitigations	Subgroup recommendations
Pre-tendering phase	Needs assessment and market analysis	• Lack of adequate needs assessment • Influence of external actors on officials' decisions • Informal agreement on contracts	• Procurement of inadequate products and quantities that do not meet the actual needs of the project.	✓ Market analysis can be based on records of past procurement activity and externally validated.	❖ Market analysis should be mandated and made available for consultation in a public version after the award decision. ❖ Annual plans for public procurement units should be disclosed through CompraNet, to promote certainty in purchase and investment plans.
Pre-tendering phase	Planning and budgeting	• Poor procurement planning • Procurement is not aligned with the overall investment decision-making process • Failure to budget realistically or deficiency in the budget	• Incorrect budget planning can lead to inefficient investment decisions.	✓ Planning can be conducted based on records of past procurement activity and externally validated.	
Pre-tendering phase	Development of specifications/ requirements	• Technical specifications are tailored for a specific company • Selection criteria are not objectively defined and are not established in advance • Unnecessary samples of goods and services are requested • Buying information on the project specifications	• The selected company is not the most suitable and results do not meet the needs.	✓ Specifications can be easily taken from previous tenders. ✓ Evaluation criteria can be predetermined and objectively applied in an evaluation module.	
Pre-tendering phase	Choice of procurement procedure	• Lack of proper justification for the use of noncompetitive procedures • Abuse of noncompetitive procedures on the basis of legal exceptions: contract splitting, abuse of extreme emergency, nonsupported modifications	• The procedure excludes contractors that could have carried out the project more efficiently.	✓ Exceptions to open processes can be made publicly available and are therefore minimised.	
Tendering phase	Request for proposal/bid	• Absence of public notice for the invitation to bid • Evaluation and award criteria are not announced • Procurement information is not disclosed or made public	• Insufficient transparency limits competition.	✓ Tender documents are all publicly available. ✓ Evaluation criteria may be automated with the evaluation module.	❖ Publication of public versions of bid proposals submitted by potential suppliers should be mandated. ❖ Approval by the Ministry of Finance and of the Institute of Social Security should be conditional on suppliers meeting their tax and social security obligations.
Tendering phase	Bid submission	• Lack of competition or cases of collusive bidding (cover bidding, bid suppression, bid rotation, market allocation)	• Lack of competition or collusive bidding may exclude the lowest-cost or most efficient bidders.	✓ Physical contact with suppliers is limited during tender phase.	
Tendering phase	Bid evaluation	• Conflict of interest and corruption in the evaluation process, through: • familiarity with bidders over time • personal interests such as gifts or future/additional employment • no effective implementation of the "four-eyes principle"	• Corruption in the evaluation process leads to an inefficient choice of contractors.	✓ Evaluation modules can standardise the bid review process. ✓ Evaluation documents are available for third-party scrutiny.	
Tendering phase	Contract award	• Vendors fail to disclose accurate cost or pricing data in their price proposals, resulting in a higher contract price (i.e. invoice mark-ups, channel stuffing) • Conflict of interest and corruption in the approval process (i.e. no effective separation of financial, contractual and project authorities) • Lack of access to records on the procedure	• Corruption in the contracting phase leads to higher contract prices.	✓ Bids are submitted electronically as open data. ✓ Approvals can be separated between roles in the system, ensuring separation of interests. ✓ All records are stored and available to accountable stakeholders.	
Post-award Phase	Contract management/ performance	• Abuses by the supplier in performing the contract, in particular in relation to its quality, price and timing: • substantial changes in contract conditions to allow more time and/or higher prices for the bidder • product substitution or sub-standard work or service that do not meet contract specifications • theft of new assets before delivery to end user or before being recorded • insufficient supervision by public officials and/or collusion between contractors and supervising officials • choice of subcontractors and partners is not done transparently or they are not held accountable.	• Inefficiencies arise from mismanagement of contracts. • Quality and delivery of products can be negatively affected, leading to delays, lower quality, and differences between specification and the delivered product.	✓ Contract milestones are logged and monitored within the system. ✓ Contract compliance records for suppliers are then available for other contracting authorities to review.	❖ Clear responsibilities for information registry obligations as well as audit mechanisms should be defined, to ensure data quality. ❖ Forbid the deletion of documents from the CompraNet system in order to keep a registry of all document versions within the tool (including who uploaded the document, when it was uploaded or modified, and which changes were made). ❖ Allow subcontracting management and supervision of transfer of collection rights. ❖ Conduct monitoring of contract execution. ❖ Enable e-government system interconnection (i.e. with the Ministry of Finance and with revenue authorities).
Post-award Phase	Order and payment	• Insufficient separation of financial duties and/or lack of supervision of public officials, leading to: • false accounting and cost misallocation or cost migration between contracts • late payment of invoices • false or duplicate invoicing for goods and services not supplied and for interim payment in advance of entitlement.	• Non-transparent invoicing and payment processes can provide opportunities for inefficient accounting and payment delays.	✓ Orders, delivery and payment can all be managed by the system. ✓ Catalogue systems can monitor stock levels.	

Source: (OECD, 2016[6]).

An effective response to the many risks mentioned above requires applying a number of different tactics in a co-ordinated fashion. Used appropriately, e-procurement can mitigate many of these risks. However, that will require a reassessment of the way technology is used within the Mexican system, and the supporting mechanisms that are necessary for it to be effective. That may involve developing a system that goes beyond simply providing access to government procurement documentation and instead offers a systematic approach to procurement. Mechanisms for integrity risk mitigation should be introduced hand in hand with efforts to increase the efficiency and effectiveness of the public procurement system. Focusing on the efficiency and effectiveness of the system as a key objective for e-procurement will improve public procurement practices and reduce opportunities for corruption throughout the procurement cycle.

As noted earlier, the introduction of CompraNet resulted in substantial benefits to public procurement in Mexico and increased the efficiency and transparency of the federal system. Through consultation with stakeholders, SFP identified the need to upgrade CompraNet to deliver further benefits. An inclusive review process was then established to identify the future direction for CompraNet to meet the needs of the system's broad array of stakeholders.

SFP convened stakeholders in a well-defined, co-ordinated governance structure

The OECD Recommendation of the Council on Public Procurement calls for member countries to "provide opportunities for direct involvement of relevant external stakeholders in the procurement system". The delivery of an e-procurement reform programme is a project with a multitude of stakeholders, each with different and often conflicting interests. The level of stakeholder engagement and participation in the CompraNet project provides an example of how an organised approach to collaboration within an appropriate governance structure can lead to a broad consensus and high levels of acceptance, or "buy-in".

An inclusive governance structure will help define and implement transformational reforms

In February 2017, the Ministry of Public Administration, through its Unit of Open Government and International Co-operation Policies (*Unidad de Políticas de Apertura Gubernamental y Cooperación Internacional*, UPAGCI), along with a series of constitutional anti-corruption reforms, commissioned the Plural Working Group on Public Procurement (the "Working Group"). This was established to investigate the enhancement of CompraNet, with the participation of leading figures from business, civil society and the public sector. The Working Group's goal was to build consensus on the development and expansion of the CompraNet system. The OECD was invited to play the role of Technical Secretariat for the project and draft a report providing recommendations based on the perspectives of the stakeholder groups and best practices in e-procurement from across member countries, building on its experience and technical knowledge. To this end, the OECD invited peer experts from countries with relevant experience in recent e-procurement implementation projects and successful reforms (i.e. Chile and Colombia).

A governance structure was established by SFP to oversee the process of collecting stakeholder feedback and input for the project. The project is headed by the Working Group, chaired by the Minister of Public Administration, with administrative responsibilities held by SFP, and with the OECD providing input and co-ordination as part of its Technical Secretariat role. Within the Working Group, six different groups were established to analyse specific interest areas (the Subgroups). They were made up of representatives from managerial levels of government, business (represented by chambers of commerce as well as by business owners and employees), civil society organisations (CSOs), the National Institute of Transparency, Information Disclosure and Protection of Personal Data (INAI), the Federal Economic Competition Commission (*Comisión Federal de Competencia Económica*, COFECE), and the National Institute for Entrepreneurs (INADEM). All Subgroup members participated in the Working Group to provide updates and direction. Other non-member actors consulted during OECD's fact-finding Mission were the Ministry of Finance, the National Anti-Corruption System, the Superior Audit Institution and representatives from operational levels of government.

Figure 1.3. Organisation chart for the Plural Working Group on Public Procurement

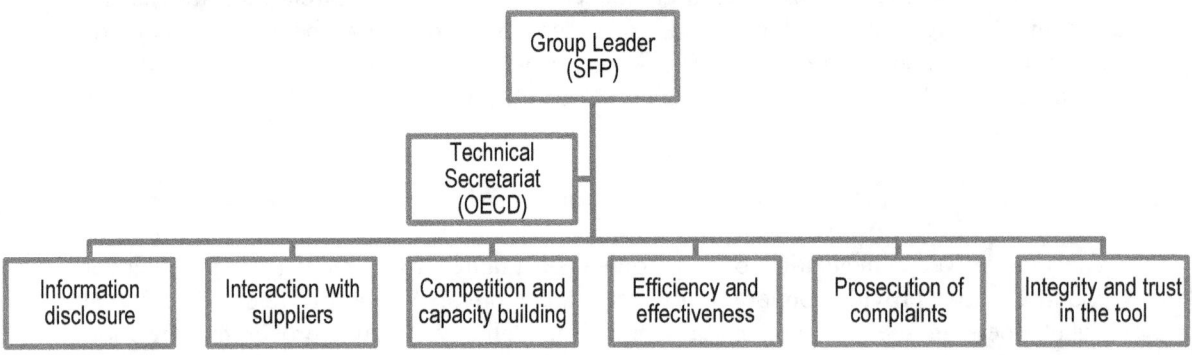

Source: Information provided courtesy of SFP.

As the main interface for public procurement between the federal government and the business community, CompraNet plays a central role in ensuring the effective and transparent operation of public procurement. Developing a strategy for CompraNet involves many interested parties. The involvement of this group of key stakeholders in this significant initiative is in line with the OECD's public procurement recommendations and represents best practice in government-led consensus building.

> **Box 1.3. OECD's Recommendation of the Council on Public Procurement – principle on participation**
>
> VI. RECOMMENDS that Adherents foster transparent and effective stakeholder participation.
>
> To this end, Adherents should:
>
> i) Develop and follow a standard process when formulating changes to the public procurement system. Such standard process should promote public consultations, **invite the comments of the private sector and civil society**, ensure the publication of the results of the consultation phase and explain the options chosen, all in a transparent manner.
>
> ii) Engage in **transparent and regular dialogues with suppliers and business associations** to present public procurement objectives and to assure a correct understanding of markets. Effective communication should be conducted to provide potential vendors with a better understanding of the country's needs, and government buyers with information to develop more realistic and effective tender specifications by better understanding market capabilities. Such interactions should be subject to due fairness, transparency and integrity safeguards, which vary depending on whether an active procurement process is ongoing. Such interactions should also be adapted to ensure that foreign companies participating in tenders receive transparent and effective information.
>
> iii) Provide opportunities for direct involvement of relevant external stakeholders in the procurement system with a view to increase transparency and integrity while assuring an adequate level of scrutiny, provided that confidentiality, equal treatment and other legal obligations in the procurement process are maintained.
>
> *Source*: (OECD, 2015[9]).

During the first meeting of the Working Group, the framework for the Subgroups, including topics to be covered and participants, were reviewed and approved. The following six areas had already been identified by SFP as key possibilities for improving the CompraNet system. Subgroup leaders were appointed by SFP according to their expertise and ability to lead a consensus within a given field. Working Group members were then invited to participate within a particular group, depending on their interests. The themes selected were: information disclosure, interaction with suppliers, competition and capacity building, efficiency and effectiveness in CompraNet, prosecution of complaints, and integrity and trust in the tool. The following table provides an overview of the makeup of the Subgroups, and the themes each was to discuss.

Table 1.1. Subgroup themes and objectives

Topic	Key issue	Participants	Themes covered
1. Information disclosure	CompraNet discloses all information relevant for users	Journalists, CSOs, suppliers, INAI, industry (chambers of commerce), SFP	Availability, accessibility, opportunity, usefulness, accuracy of information
2. Interaction with suppliers	Streamlining the tools for engaging suppliers through e-procurement	Industry (chambers of commerce)	Functionality enhancements, transparency, anti-corruption, statistics, professionalisation
3. Competition and capacity building	Encourage the use of electronic means throughout the public procurement cycle	Public officials, tendering contractors and suppliers	Robustness of platform, reducing participation costs, reducing administrative costs, limiting direct contact between participants
4. Efficiency and effectiveness in CompraNet	Alternative solutions and measures to improve the platform	CSOs	Analysis of applicable regulations, background of CompraNet, practical operation of the platform, accessibility of processes and results
5. Prosecution of complaints	Processing of complaints focused on creating confidence and credibility in the business sector	Public officials and industry (chambers of commerce)	Analysis of current process flow, diagnosis of options to improve SIDEC (SFP's complaint system) and CompraNet (best practices), technological update proposal
6. Integrity and trust in the tool	Identify actions that increase trust in CompraNet, ensuring accurate and timely information	CSOs	Integrity of the information contained in CompraNet, trust in processes related to CompraNet, mechanisms and actions external to CompraNet that affect its reliability and integrity

Source: Courtesy of information provided by SFP.

The Working Group meetings were held periodically, convened and led by the SFP to monitor and gather updates on the progress made by the Subgroups. From the work done by Subgroups to develop recommendations between February and July 2017, a total of 21 recommendations were presented, covering a diverse range of issues. These included implementing international standards for classifying goods and services, the adoption of approved formats or templates to systematise information, and the public disclosure of information for additional phases of the procurement cycle. These recommendations were used by the OECD as the basis for this report. A final version was reviewed at the meeting of the OECD Working Party of Leading Practitioners on Public Procurement (16-17 October 2017) and approved at the seventh Working Group on Public Procurement meeting in November 2017.

Figure 1.4. Summary of Plenary Meetings from February to November 2017

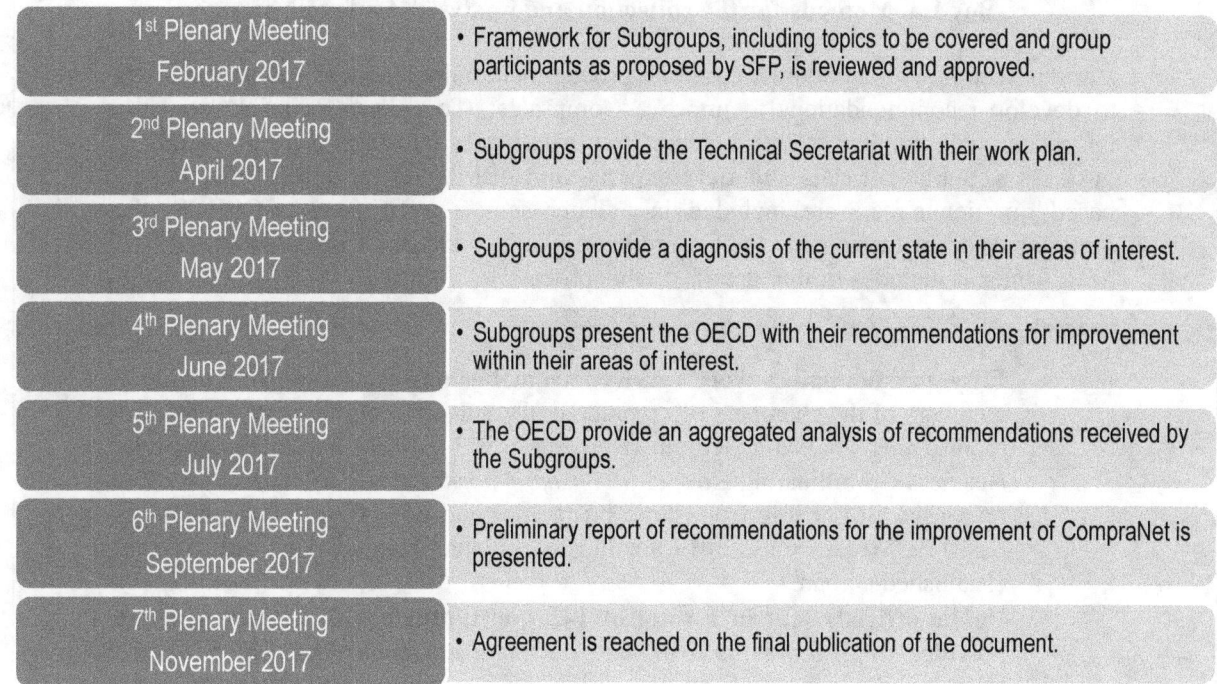

Source: Courtesy of information provided by SFP.

Involving stakeholder groups in the project as part of a well-defined, co-ordinated project structure has helped to ensure a collaborative and inclusive process. Working Group meetings are used to update all parties involved on the progress made and to arrive at agreement on the direction of the project.

Surveys of users helped subgroups develop an aligned vision for the future of CompraNet

The six Subgroups developed a series of recommendations for the advancement of CompraNet, each choosing what they considered to be the most appropriate methods for collecting and analysing information. Diverse stakeholder groups helped shape these analyses, including representatives from CSOs, field experts and academia, journalists, autonomous constitutional bodies such as COFECE, and the Superior Audit Institution (*Auditoría Superior de la Federación*, ASF), which is accountable to the Legislature (*Cámara de Diputados*). The groups used a variety of methods, including surveys, documentary reviews and examining international best practices. Survey participants were selected from user groups including contracting authorities, public officials, and current and prospective suppliers.

> **Box 1.4. Methods for the collection and analysis of information**
>
> Various sectors with an interest in public procurement helped collect and analyse data to develop recommendations to improve CompraNet. To collect feedback from the largest possible number of stakeholders, web-based questionnaires were prepared for businesses, public officials and field experts, and distributed on a web link. Paper-based questionnaires were included in a letter sent to officials of COFECE, the Superior Audit Institution and the Co-ordination Unit of Internal Control Bodies of the SFP. Annex B includes further details on this process.
>
> In total:
>
> - **Fifty questionnaires were received from businesses.** Participants included members of the chambers of commerce, the construction industry, a chamber representing small and medium-sized enterprises (SMEs), and members of the Business Co-ordinating Council (*Consejo Coordinador Empresarial*). Of the responses, 36% came from large businesses and 64% from SMEs; 44% are based in Mexico City, 50% are located outside Mexico City, and 6% are established abroad.
> - **Public officials sent in a total of 148 questionnaires.** A contact database provided by SFP was used to send out these questionnaires. The SFP also encouraged participation by presenting the questionnaire to public officials. The contact database classified contracting authorities into three different tiers, based on the amount of their spending: 20% of the officials surveyed work in one of the 30 entities or government agencies that spend most public resources on their contracting processes.
> - **Five questionnaires were received from CSO experts and eight questionnaires from journalists.** This did not provide a sufficiently large sample to allow for in-depth analysis.
> - **Questionnaires were sent to COFECE, the Superior Audit Institution, and the Co-ordination Unit of Internal Control Bodies of the SFP.** Officials from these groups were consulted as a result either of their direct involvement in the system, or their use of information collected by the system. Responses were received in an official letter addressed to the Technical Secretariat.
>
> *Source:* (Technical Secretariat, 2017[10]).

Once the surveys were conducted, and all other processes to collect and analye information had concluded, the subgroups presented to the Technical Secretariat their diagnosis and recommendations for enhancing CompraNet. The recommendations were presented using a unified format that included a cost-benefit analysis and an analysis of legal implications. In total, 51 recommendations were received, which, after they were analysed and aggregated, were consolidated into 21 proposals for improvement.

The recommendations collected by the OECD were analysed and compared with the OECD's own experience of successful practices in other countries to develop the final recommendations in this report. The perspectives of subgroup members, and the stakeholder groups they represent, were consolidated into a vision statement to help guide the system going forward.

A vision statement for CompraNet aims to unite stakeholders behind common goals

An effective vision statement can align stakeholders behind a set of common outcomes. Describing the system in terms of outcomes, as opposed to inputs and technical specifications, can help stakeholders understand how the system will deliver for them, giving SFP the necessary flexibility to determine how those outcomes can be achieved.

More than 20 years have passed since the original approach to the development of the e-procurement system was established in the Information Technology (IT) Development Programme 1995-2000. When it was set up, in 1996, CompraNet was part of an effort to modernise Mexico's federal public administration, using information and communications technology (ICT) to increase the quality of, and access to, public procurement. The declared goal of CompraNet's first Vision Statement was to establish an accessible system where tenders could be published, offers registered, and results and follow-up on awards published for all public tenders relating to the acquisition of goods, services and public works by the federal public administration.

Box 1.5. IT Development Programme 1995-2000

3.1.5 Priority goals

For the year 2000:

[...]

The procedures of private companies with agencies of the federal public administration, such as those relating to their registration and those related to government procurement, may be made through networks from a terminal, a digital telephone or a personal computer.

Initial target: By 1997, a network system will be in place for the publication of bidding rules, bid registration, publication of results and monitoring of allotments, where all public tenders for the procurement of goods, services and public works will be registered in the central public administration. This system must be accessible from all Mexico's state capitals.

Source: (DOF, 1996$_{[11]}$).

The work of the Subgroups has identified a number of areas where CompraNet can be improved to meet the needs of its many stakeholders. The recommendations ranged from technical adjustments that would improve the functioning of the current system to more substantial changes that involve integrating the system with other government platforms and expanding the scope to other stages of the procurement cycle.

To overcome the challenges identified in the current system, the vision statement can provide a common set of expectations to guide the improvement and modification of the CompraNet system. According to Bain, a vision statement should outline the "objectives and (the) approach to reach those objectives", while inspiring civil servants "to work more productively by providing focus and common goals" and can also "guide decision making" (Bain & Company, 2015[12]). Components of an effective vision statement development process include the following (United Nations Relief and Works Agency (UNRWA), 2009[13]):

- *Engage the right people in the process*: Make sure that the right stakeholders are involved in developing the vision statement.
- *Create and use a process that ensures full participation, openness, creativity and efficiency*: The process is more likely to be effective if there is a plan and a process; this may require the involvement of an external facilitator.
- *Do the "cosmetic" work off line*: Rather than involving the whole group in the finer details of the vision statement, it is best to fine-tune the document separately and present a polished product to the group.
- *Talk to the outliers*: If there are individuals or groups who do not agree with the vision statement, consult with them to ensure they are committed to the vision, or explore ways to connect the vision to their interests and needs.
- *Reconvene the group to review the draft vision statement*: This should not require lengthy scrutiny by the whole group, but should discuss whether the group is in agreement on the general direction of the document, rather than approves every word.
- *Communicate the vision and begin to make it a reality*: A vision is just a picture for the future without solid goals and action plans; the next step is to develop those. The vision itself can be brought to life by using creative people on the team to develop images, metaphors and stories.

As part of the work by the members of the Working Group, a document was developed to outline the vision for the future of the electronic public procurement system in Mexico, which was then amended to align with best practice.

Box 1.6. Vision for Mexico's federal government e-procurement system

More than 20 years after the launch of CompraNet, the Plural Working Group on Public Procurement convened by the Ministry of Public Administration has had the opportunity to review the achievements of the e-procurement system. New foundations for Mexico's federal government e-procurement system can harness the energy of our diverse economy, increase co-operation between the public, private and social sectors, and promote prosperity with an efficient, effective and transparent system governing the use of federal funds, subject to the regulations on acquisitions, public works and public-private partnerships.[1]

In developing a better e-procurement system, the Plural Working Group on Public Procurement recognises the opportunities provided by digital technology to enable a fully transactional system that supports the whole public procurement cycle, from planning through tendering and award (contracting), to payment and contract management, as well as subsequent monitoring and auditing.

The success of the Plural Working Group on Public Procurement has been the result of the ability of different sectors, namely CSOs, business leaders and federal institutions, to adapt to changing circumstances. Our economy and societies are moving towards a democratic state that calls on all social actors to be accountable and responsive. The members of the Plural Working Group on Public Procurement are committed to deepening our co-operation, based on our shared vision of achieving stability and prosperity for our peoples through good governance.

To this end, we aim to make Mexico's federal government e-procurement system:

1. **transactional:** The entire public procurement cycle will be managed electronically and establish complete flows connecting each of the steps automatically.
2. **standardised:** The entire public procurement cycle will conform to specifications and approved pre-established formats and adopt internationally accepted contracting data standards.
3. **transparent:** The e-procurement system will be the only access point for publishing information of the government procurement cycle using federal public funds, regardless of whether the case is part of an ordinary process or an exception. The system facilitates compliance with data and document disclosure principles as well as transparency duties.
4. **trustworthy:** The information uploaded to the system will be accurate, complete, updated and secured under strict protocols. All versions and updates of the documents referring to the public procurement cycle and uploaded to the platform will be kept, including modifying agreements, indicating the date and time of update as well as the official responsible for the information. Information and documents in the platform should be recognised as official and may be used in any legal proceeding.
5. **interconnected:** The system will offer interconnection between the processes of the procurement cycle as well as between government information systems (e-government), including those of budget and revenue agencies.

6. **co-ordinated:** The various entities and user units of the system will use it as a tool to ease co-ordination and facilitate consolidated purchases looking for the best market conditions and the standardisation of the procurement process. The system will include modules that allow for public procurement strategies such as reverse auctions and framework agreements.
7. **user-friendly:** The system is designed to offer users clarity on the available information and where to find it, as well as quick access to the system and high-speed navigation, avoiding too many system-interaction rules. A help desk provides useful advice to users, with sufficient numbers of qualified staff to address users' needs.
8. **instrumental for users:** The platform provides information for both public servants and the social and private sectors, as necessary. It will help them in the following tasks: analysing public procurement and the performance of those involved in such activity; making decisions to participate in procurement processes; defining public policies and improvement initiatives for public procurement; supporting audit and control tasks, and carrying out investigations and analyses of procurement outcomes, including the production of statistics and indicators. The platform will also facilitate the preparation of market research and Annual Plans of acquisitions, leases and services, as well as public works, so they can be published in a timely manner with updated information and provide useful input for the industry. The system's Registry of suppliers, including supplier profiles, shareholders, history of performance in public procurement and illicit actions, will contribute to informed decision making by procurement officials.
9. **accountable:** The system links to citizen complaint mechanisms set up for the complete procurement cycle and includes an updated registry of suppliers that have been sanctioned. It contributes data and evidence to review and evaluation mechanisms performed by different authorities (i.e. audit bodies, and transparency and competition authorities) to improve public procurement operations.
10. **dynamic and innovative:** A focus on process innovation will help the system introduce new information-management methodologies in procurement for public works, goods and services, based on knowledge from previous experiences, opinion and feedback from users, and guided by international best practices.
11. **geared towards economic competition.** The system encourages competition, free concurrence and reduces entry barriers, transaction and administrative costs for all types of users. The system will be publicly accessible. All information will be available for consultation in its public version in a timely manner and in a way that does not restrict economic competition or negatively affect the efficiency of public procurement by facilitating collusion and bid rigging.
12. **exemplary.** The federal e-procurement system will be a good practice for all other public e-procurement systems in Mexico to follow, such as those to be developed by states, municipalities and public entities subject to different procurement regimes.

Source: Plural Working Group on Public Procurement.

This vision statement is based on the Subgroups' efforts to identify the system's current challenges and to collect opinions on the attributes of a system that will work for all stakeholders. It focuses on developing an e-procurement solution that operates as part of an efficient and effective public procurement system. For any future plans or projects that aim to develop or improve CompraNet, this statement can be used as a point of reference for capturing the goals and ambitions of all stakeholders.

Note

[1] As of the time of drafting this vision, these regulations were the Law on Public Sector Acquisitions, Leases and Services (LAASSP), the Law on Public Works and Related Services (LOPRSM), and the Law for Public-Private Partnerships, as well as the secondary regulations derived therefrom.

References

Asian Development Bank (2013), *e-Government Procurement Handbook*, https://www.adb.org/sites/default/files/institutional-document/34064/files/e-government-procurement-handbook.pdf (accessed on 20 November 2017). [3]

Bain & Company (2015), *Management Tools - Mission and Vision Statements*, http://www.bain.com/publications/articles/management-tools-mission-and-vision-statements.aspx (accessed on 25 September 2017). [12]

DOF (1996), *Programa de Desarrollo Informático 1995-2000*. [11]

Dussauge, M. (2010), *Combate a la corrupción y rendición de cuentas: avances, limitaciones, pendientes y retrocesos*, El Colegio de México. [1]

Marván, M. (2015), *La corrupción en México: percepción, práctica y sentido ético*, Instituto de Investigaciones Jurídicas - UNAM. [5]

OECD (2016), *Preventing Corruption in Public Procurement*, OECD Publishing, http://www.oecd.org/gov/ethics/Corruption-in-Public-Procurement-Brochure.pdf (accessed on 14 September 2017). [6]

OECD (2016), *Survey on Public Procurement*, OECD Publishing. [8]

OECD (2015), "OECD Recommendation of the Council on Public Procurement", https://www.oecd.org/gov/ethics/OECD-Recommendation-on-Public-Procurement.pdf (accessed on 14 September 2017). [9]

Pardo, M. (2009), *La modernización administrativa en México, 1940-2006*, El Colegio de México. [2]

Procurement Harmonization Project of the Asian Development Bank, T. (2004), "Electronic Government Procurement Roadmap", http://siteresources.worldbank.org/INFORMATIONANDCOMMUNICATIONANDTECHNOLOGIES/Resources/eGPRoadMap.pdf (accessed on 14 September 2017). [4]

Technical Secretariat (2017), *Questionnaire for Businesses*, https://docs.google.com/forms/d/1UUZwo5n7yJ6fE_WeqVkyxaq9HmVwf7rJBooKI2t2PHQ/edit?c=0&w=1#responses. [10]

The World Bank; Schapper, P. (2007), "Corruption and Technology in Public Procurement", http://siteresources.worldbank.org/INFORMATIONANDCOMMUNICATIONANDTECHNOLOGIES/Resources/CorruptionversusTechnologyinPublicProcurement.pdf (accessed on 14 September 2017). [7]

United Nations Relief and Works Agency (UNRWA) (2009), "How to Create a Shared Vision Statement", https://www.unrwa.org/userfiles/file/leading_4_the_future/module1/How%20to%20Create%20a%20Shared%20Vision%20Statement.pdf (accessed on 11 September 2017). [13]

Chapter 2. Upgrading CompraNet to a system that delivers for all stakeholders

E-procurement systems are used throughout OECD countries to ensure that public procurement activity is efficient, effective, transparent and accountable. To ensure that the e-procurement system can deliver the anticipated benefits, it is imperative to incorporate system re-design within a broader approach to reform. This involves identifying the supporting mechanisms (including legislation, policy, training and infrastructure) that are necessary for the system to succeed. In this chapter, CompraNet's scope, functionality and application by users are measured against global trends in e-procurement, with a view to developing a system that meets the unique needs of different users, increases competition and returns value for money.

The initial push to implement e-procurement systems in OECD member countries over the past 15 to 20 years was directed towards building centralised systems for publishing public procurement information. As a result, the focus for the majority of member countries during that period was on developing national, cross-governmental systems that cover the core aspects of the sourcing process, namely from the call for tender until the award of a contract, allowing contracting authorities to manage the rest of the process through stand-alone systems and processes (OECD, 2016[1]).

The focus on investment in e-procurement systems has gradually shifted away from this original purpose towards developing systems that help increase efficiency and effectiveness in procurement practices. The next phase of the development of e-procurement systems, an approach championed by the OECD and the European Commission, is likely to focus on advances in the following areas:

- taking opportunities to increase efficiency and standardisation by extending the e-procurement system to cover the whole public procurement cycle
- integrating the system with other e-government technologies, such as public finance management, budgeting and service delivery processes, to optimise public resources through better transmission of information, automation and increased accountability.

Although it can handle some of the required features of modern e-procurement systems, CompraNet does not yet support the full digital management of the procurement cycle. So far, the system only covers those aspects of the cycle related to the publication of tender documents, the submission of bids and the awarding of contracts. SFP has however, attempted to expand its scope over time to include additional processes in the procurement cycle.

However, the current system faces various challenges in ensuring consistent, systematised and transparent adherence to procurement legislation. These issues are the result not only of weaknesses in the system, but inconsistencies in the processes used by contracting authorities and disparities in the capabilities of Mexico's procurement workforce.

Reinforcing CompraNet's role in enabling public procurement reform

SFP should consider aligning e-procurement with a broad reform programme

Implementing an e-procurement system can encounter many different hurdles. As a start, the system should be part of a multifaceted programme in concert with other aspects of procurement reform (such as legal and policy settings, and development of the private sector). This requires an e-procurement strategy that is suited to the economic environment and provides solid foundations for the platform itself.

During the OECD fact-finding missions, it became clear that stakeholder groups raised issues with public procurement that extended beyond the technical and functionality requirements of CompraNet. In addition to implementing recommendations related to system changes and improvements, SFP should also identify ways to overcome other barriers to the effective operation of the process, including the following challenges:

- **Procurement practitioners do not comply with procurement guidelines, and do not always upload the required information:** Either because of lack of capacity in working with CompraNet or insufficient procurement capacity in general, procurement practitioners may require additional support and guidance to execute their roles effectively. This may be related to the use of the system or to the enforcement of procurement processes, policies or legislation.

- **Exemptions to procurement legislation may not be consistently applied:** There are cases where a contracting authority can legitimately refrain from conducting an open tender process, such as in cases of emergency where goods and services are required within a narrow timeframe, or where it can be established that the goods or service are only available from a single supplier. Nevertheless, staff operating procurement processes do not always comply with policies on the selection of procurement procedures. According to SFP, as of 2017, 68% of all contracts were awarded directly (accounting for 25% of public funds assigned through contracting) while only 18% of contracts were conducted through a public tender process (accounting for 64% of the monetary value). A large number of lower-value transactions are thus not subject to competitive procedures.
- **The format of tender documents varies widely:** Substantial variations in tender documents can require additional time and effort from contracting authorities, businesses responding to tenders and oversight institutions or "social witnesses"[2]. Standardisation will not only allow procurement practitioners and businesses to develop documents more efficiently, but help to streamline requirements across government, including contract terms, general specifications and reporting requirements. Standardising contracts will also make the analysis of procurement data easier, by harmonising variables between all procurement processes.

The 2016 OECD Survey on Public Procurement suggests that the main challenges faced by contracting authorities in OECD countries in using e-procurement systems are an organisational culture that is not as innovative as it could be (57%), limited ICT knowledge and skills (40%) and limited familiarity with the economic opportunities that e-procurement systems can offer (37%).

Figure 2.1. Challenges facing contracting authorities in OECD countries in using e-procurement

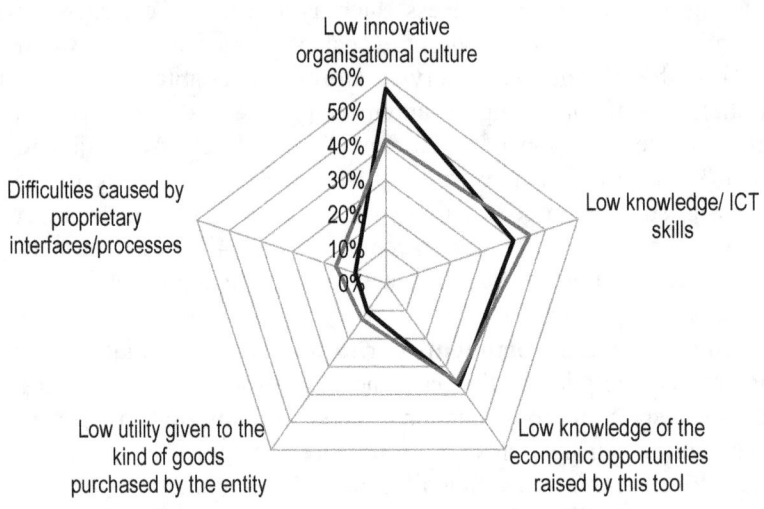

Source: (OECD, 2016[1]).

Technological change must be part of a comprehensive strategy that removes barriers to the e-procurement system. Without the accompanying reforms, it may not achieve the benefits hoped for. Benefits yielded by e-procurement are usually a result of stronger management and co-ordination facilitated by technology, rather than of technology *per se* (Asian Development Bank, 2013[2]).

According to a study carried out by the European Bank for Reconstruction and Development on implementing diverse e-procurement solutions, these five pillars are the essential elements of an e-procurement strategy:

- **Government and institutional leadership:** Government sets the vision for what is to be achieved; the operational implementation must then be owned or co-ordinated by one agency to achieve commonality of standards and approaches.
- **Management, legislation, regulation and policy:** E-procurement is a business rather than a technological system, and requires strong legislative and management frameworks to be successful. Changes to the e-procurement system will result in amendments to the processes and policies surrounding government procurement, including revised audit and compliance regimes and improved management information on all aspects of procurement. These changes must be understood and prepared for in advance of any modifications to the system.
- **Private sector activation:** An e-procurement strategy needs to be mindful of, and consult with, the private sector if it is to be effective for both supply and demand. Any engagement strategy should consider how to communicate with

businesses to build the case for system changes and prepare users for changes in functionality.

- **Infrastructure and web services:** The success of a government e-procurement system depends on the extent to which all government procurement practitioners and all actual and potential suppliers to government can access it. In addition, an e-procurement strategy must be anchored by other IT management practices, such as data management, security management and access management.
- **Functionality and standards:** The level of functionality required will depend on the types of procurement transactions the system is used for (conversely, the more complex the transaction, the simpler the system requirements). Selecting open or proprietary technical standards is a complex decision that involves many factors.

Figure 2.2. Facets of an e-procurement Strategy

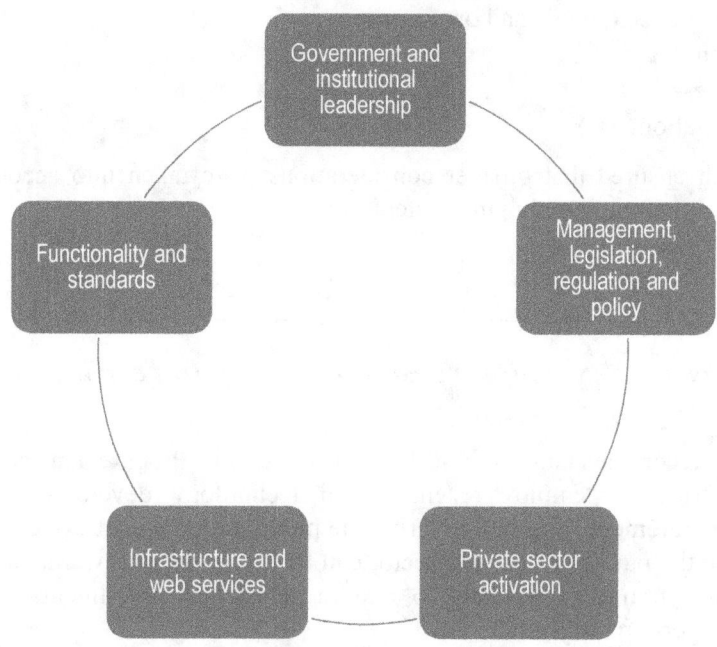

Source: (EBRD; UNCITRAL, 2015[3]).

E-procurement can play a significant role in public procurement reform, but it will not necessarily remedy poor procurement practice and it may not solve underlying problems in public procurement operations. Poor practices can quite easily be perpetuated through e-procurement (OECD, 2011[4]), and setting up an e-procurement system cannot ensure that processes are open, fair and appropriate to the needs of each procurement, nor replace the need to ensure that practitioners are well-trained, capable and act with integrity.

Different countries take various approaches, but the underlying objectives remain similar and aligned with priorities of public governance.

> **Box 2.1. A comprehensive e-procurement strategy in Slovakia**
>
> Four objectives were identified to develop an e-procurement strategy in Slovakia for the use and implementation of the national e-procurement system:
>
> - reducing public spending
> - increasing transparency
> - promoting fair competition
> - simplifying and accelerating the procurement process.
>
> To achieve these objectives in a sustainable way, it was clear that activities involving the electronic platform itself would need to be supported by other initiatives. Each action was assessed in relation to the dimensions of the procurement system that would be affected, from the following options:
>
> - governance (people and organisation)
> - technology
> - processes
> - legislation.
>
> This approach ensured that broader considerations were taken into account for each change that was required within the system.
>
> *Source:* (OECD, 2017[5]).

Upgrading CompraNet alongside e-Government reforms can lead to a fully transactional procure-to-pay system

The OECD's Recommendation of the Council on Public Procurement calls on OECD member countries to "employ recent digital technology developments that allow integrated e-procurement solutions covering the public procurement cycle". Enhancing e-procurement in the public and private sector can be the first step towards more integrated systems. Such a transition is likely to require significant investment, and should be viewed as a longer-term objective.

Figure 2.3. Illustration of the evolution of technology in procurement over time

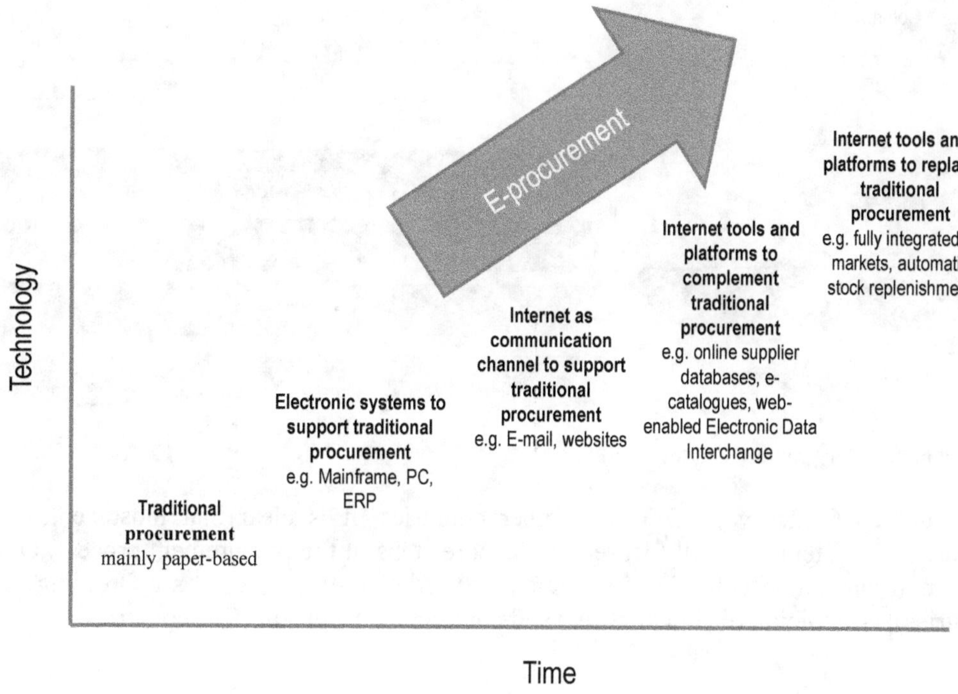

[Chart showing Technology (y-axis) vs Time (x-axis) with an arrow labeled "E-procurement" pointing upward to the right, with stages:]

- **Traditional procurement** — mainly paper-based
- **Electronic systems to support traditional procurement** — e.g. Mainframe, PC, ERP
- **Internet as communication channel to support traditional procurement** — e.g. E-mail, websites
- **Internet tools and platforms to complement traditional procurement** — e.g. online supplier databases, e-catalogues, web-enabled Electronic Data Interchange
- **Internet tools and platforms to replace traditional procurement** — e.g. fully integrated e-markets, automatic stock replenishment

Source: (United Nations, 2006[6]).

The scope of CompraNet is confined to activities related to the posting of tender documents by government agencies, the management of clarifying questions, the submission of bids and the awarding of contracts. For Mexico, as in the majority of OECD countries, the original objectives for e-procurement were to increase transparency and access to tender opportunities, for both national and international businesses. For this reason, a common approach across OECD countries through the genesis of public e-procurement has been to develop web-based solutions independent of the systems used by contracting authorities. Web-based, central platforms with little integration are a simpler and less costly alternative to a system that is integrated with contracting authorities' payment systems.

Figure 2.4. Comparison of the scope of CompraNet vs. contracting authorities' systems

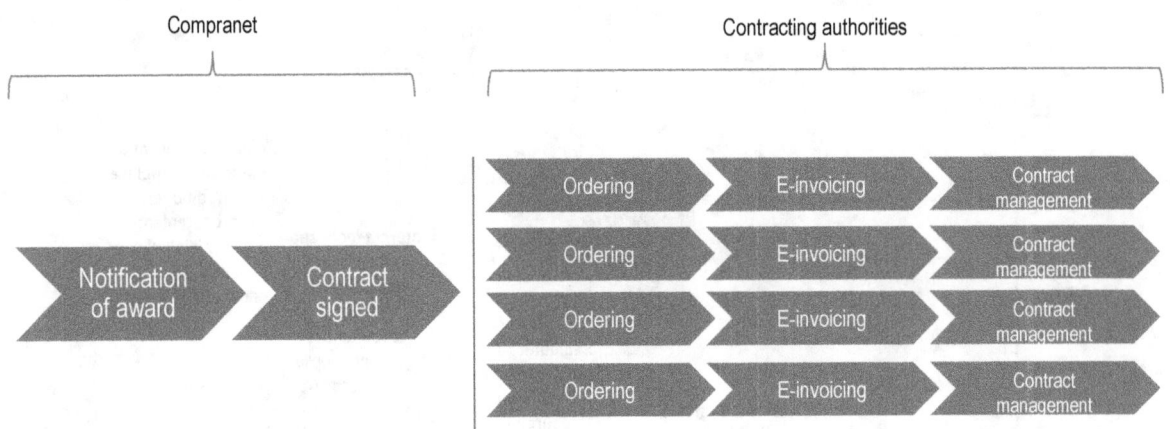

Source: Information provided courtesy of SFP.

From the 2016 survey of OECD member countries, it is clear that most central e-procurement systems are still focused on the core steps of the procurement process. Only in a small number of countries do they cover the latter stages, such as e-Ordering (six countries), e-Invoicing (eight countries) and contract management (five countries).

Figure 2.5. Functionalities of e-procurement systems in OECD countries

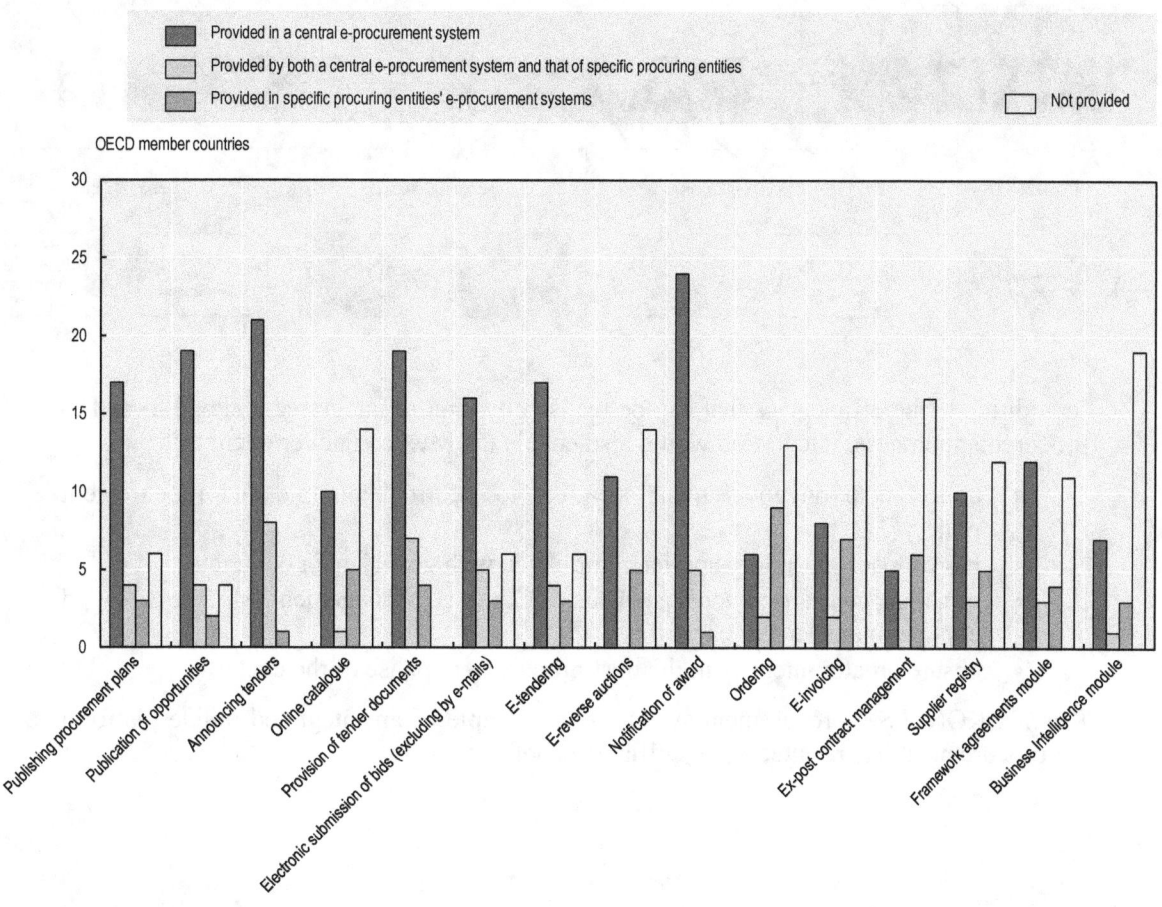

Source: (OECD, 2016[1]).

Procurement has evolved thanks to progress made possible by technological advances. What was once a paper-based function can now be digitised to a large degree. The next step in OECD countries that have not already done so will be vertical integration (i.e. integration of the central tendering platform with the finance or contract management systems of contracting authorities) resulting in a fully integrated, end-to-end procurement system.

Figure 2.6. Horizontal versus vertical integration

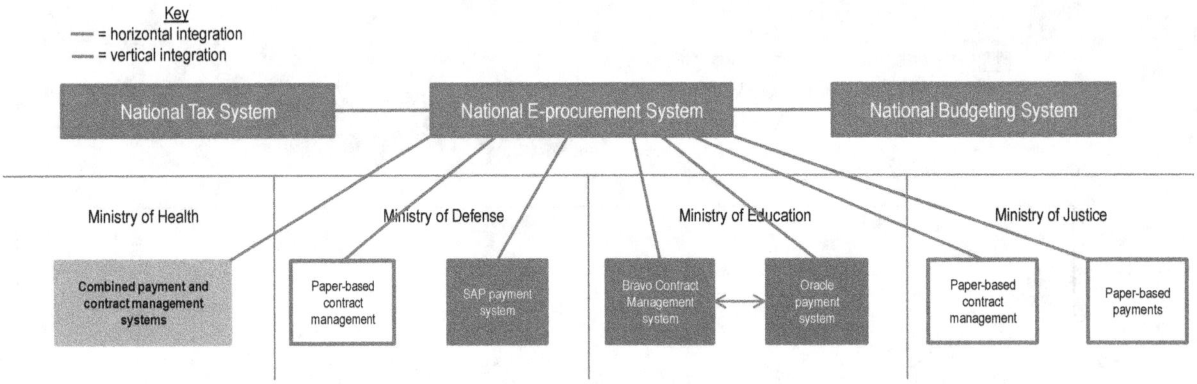

In addition to the efficiencies that can be realised by a more integrated and end-to-end e-procurement process, integration would also enable the Mexican government to:

- collect data on government spending to inform economic and procurement policy
- more closely monitor supplier compliance with government contracts
- establish centralised tools such as a Contract Management Module to build contract management capability
- ensure greater integrity in the post-procurement phase of the cycle.

Korea's KONEPS e-procurement system, one example of an integrated online platform for procurement, has resulted in quantifiable benefits.

> **Box 2.2. The integrated e-procurement system KONEPS in Korea**
>
> In Korea, the implementation of a national e-procurement system has achieved significant advances in the transparency and integrity of public procurement.
>
> In 2002, Public Procurement Services (PPS), Korea's central procurement agency, introduced a fully integrated, end-to-end procurement system called KONEPS. This system covers the entire procurement cycle electronically (including a one-time registration, tendering, contracts, inspection and payment) and related documents are exchanged online. KONEPS links about 140 external systems to share and retrieve any necessary information, and provides a one-stop service, including automatic collection of bidders' qualification data, delivery report, e-Invoicing and e-Payment. It provides information on a real-time basis.
>
> All public organisations are mandated to tender publicly through KONEPS. In 2012, over 62.7% of Korea's total public procurement (USD 106 billion) was conducted through KONEPS. In KONEPS, 45 000 public entities interact with 244 000 registered suppliers. According to PPS, the system has boosted efficiency and significantly reduced transaction costs. The system has also increased participation in public tenders and considerably improved transparency, eliminating instances of corruption by preventing illegal practices and collusive acts. For example, the Korea Fair Trade Commission runs BRIAS, a KONEPS system, an automated system that detects suspicious bid strategies. According to the integrity assessment conducted by Korea's Anti-Corruption and Civil Rights Commission, the integrity perception index of PPS has improved from 6.8 to 8.5 out of 10 since the launch of KONEPS.
>
> Use of borrowed e-Certificates was a key concern, in terms of practices that would facilitate illegal activity. To mitigate this risk, the Public Procurement Service introduced "Fingerprint Recognition e-Bidding" in 2010. Under this system, each user can tender for only one company, using a biometric security token. Fingerprint information is stored only in the concerned supplier's file, thus avoiding any controversy over the government's storage of personal biometric information. By July 2010, it was applied in all tenders carried out via KONEPS by local governments and other public organisations procuring goods, services and construction projects. In 2011, PPS launched a new service allowing the bidding process to take place via smartphones, using newly developed security tokens and applications.
>
> *Source:* (OECD, 2016[7]).

The business case for such a large-scale project as multi-agency integration may still need to be made to encourage countries to make the sizeable investment. The benefits to government of fully integrated systems are clear, yet often difficult to quantify. Among OECD countries, 66% do not measure the efficiencies/savings generated by using e-procurement (OECD, 2016[1]). Countries that have measured the savings usually focus on the time saved by increased process efficiency or, as in the case of Korea, the amount of public and private funds saved.

> **Box 2.3. Korea's system integration has cut the cost of procurement transactions**
>
> Through the shared use of government data and data interchange between KONEPS and other databases owned by public authorities, KONEPS made it possible to eliminate paper submission of business registration and tax payment certificates. For public construction tenders, bidders are no longer required to submit certificates on their past experience, because such data is electronically collected through data interchange with construction industry associations.
>
> According to a study conducted in 2009, annual transaction cost savings made possible by KONEPS amounted to KRW 9.5 trillion. Of this, KRW 1.6 trillion (EUR 1.2 billion) was saved in the public sector in reduced labour and process time, due to the streamlined, digitised work process. KRW 7.9 trillion was saved in the private sector, mainly from reduced costs for visiting public entities and obtaining required certificates and proof documents. Reductions in labour and time from streamlined and standardised procedures also contributed to the savings.
>
> *Source:* (OECD, 2015[8]).

Achieving end-to-end integration of the processes surrounding public procurement may also require horizontal integration involving linking the central e-procurement system with other government systems. OECD member countries have made limited progress in integrating procurement systems with other government platforms. According to an OECD survey, 60% of e-procurement systems are not integrated with other e-Government digital technology solutions such as budgeting, business and tax registries, social security databases, financial systems for payment, and Enterprise Resource Planning systems (OECD, 2016[1]). Integrating e-Government platforms is in line with the OECD Recommendation of the Council on Digital Government Strategies, as it enables full visibility of the use of public funds across different government departments (OECD, 2014[9]).

Efforts have been made to prepare to integrate CompraNet and the Ministry of Finance's budget system, the *Sistema de Contabilidad y Presupuesto* (SICOP). SICOP manages all payments by government agencies that involve the use of federal resources, and stores information on contracts, contractual terms, modifying agreements to contract terms, and the final amounts paid for goods, services and public works. Connecting CompraNet and SICOP would allow the e-procurement system to follow any given procurement process, from the budget assignment phase to the final payment of contracts, allowing procurement officials to avoid duplication. Information would be fed to a single system, rather than the multiple information registries now in place.

Interoperability with other national systems, such as the National Transparency Platform and the Platform of the National Anti-Corruption System, would enhance the government's ability to develop a comprehensive picture of public procurement activity. The National Transparency Platform was introduced to allow the proactive publication of information on government activity at both the federal and sub-national level, on a single platform. If CompraNet could communicate directly with this system, public procurement information entered into CompraNet could be used by the National Transparency Platform, avoiding inefficiencies of double-handling and the risk of data inconsistencies.

Similarly, the National Anti-corruption System will be used to store data used to support anti-corruption policies in Mexico, including registries of sanctioned suppliers and sanctioned public officials, and the registry of officials carrying out public procurement activities.

These systems are currently under development. It will be important that they have the capacity to exchange information with CompraNet. Linking the information in these systems with CompraNet will enable authorities across government to fight corruption in an integrated fashion.

A programme is also under way to enable interconnection between CompraNet and national tax systems. The aim is to identify businesses that are properly registered and fulfill the obligations of the Tax Revenue Agency (*Sistema de Administración Tributaria*, SAT), as well as to identify "ghost" companies and prevent them from participating in public tenders (El Financiero, 2017[10]). "Ghost" companies are used to win government tenders and receive public funds by parties that have no ability to execute the contract. Identifying and eliminating them from tender processes would reduce the waste of public funds.

Other stakeholder groups also stand to benefit from interoperability between government systems. For example, access to information on companies that participate in government tender opportunities can help competition authorities identify cases of bid rigging. By providing information on subcontracting arrangements and joint bids, CompraNet could give competition authorities better information on trends such as unusually low tenders and collusive bidding patterns further down the supply chain.

> **Box 2.4. Horizontal system integration with national finance in Colombia**
>
> As part of the transition to a new generation of the e-procurement platform in Colombia, the second phase of the *Sistema Electrónico para la Contratación Pública* (SECOP II) was expanded to integrate with the *Sistema Integrado de Información Financiera* (SIIP). This direct connection with the financial reporting system greatly increased data accuracy and transparency on spending by procurement entities. Integrating procurement and budget data eliminated risks of corruption such as the separation of financial duties, examples of false accounting and cost misallocation, and late payment of invoices.
>
> Some government entities are mandated to use the system, and some are merely encouraged to do so. To attract bodies (such as state-owned entities) that are not mandated by law to use the system, *Colombia Compra Eficiente* has developed a series of key performance indicators that measure the performance of the national procurement system in a number of categories. Each measure has a baseline result from the preceding year, to develop targets in the following areas:
>
> - value for money: includes metrics on the time required for procurement processes and savings achieved through procurement;
> - integrity and transparency in competition: includes measures on the number of contracts awarded to new suppliers and the percentage of contracts awarded through noncompetitive processes;
> - accountability: includes measures on public entities using SECOP and the percentage of awarded contracts published on SECOP;
> - risk management: features one single measure, on the percentage of contracts with modifications of time or value.
>
> *Source:* (OECD, 2016[11]).

The Korean and Colombian examples, and the trend toward increased integration, suggest the need for a comparable vision for CompraNet. Integrating it with central and government e-procurement and finance systems would be the ultimate goal.

A user-friendly system providing easily accessible, open and reliable data

Open data practices could normalise public procurement data and enhance accountability

While a large amount of information on Mexican public procurement activity is available on CompraNet, the data is not sufficiently comprehensive, and it is not available in formats that can increase accountability. The current process for achieving transparency and accountability in public procurement involves public disclosure of a large number of documents in formats such as scanned PDFs. This means that control entities and other stakeholders (e.g. auditors or the public) must invest considerable effort and resources in identifying acts of corruption. Increasing accountability requires public disclosure of high-quality data in a format that allows analysts to detect trends and exceptions.

> **Box 2.5. OECD's Recommendation of the Council on Public Procurement – principle on transparency**
>
> II. RECOMMENDS that Adherents ensure an adequate degree of transparency of the public procurement system in all stages of the procurement cycle. To this end, Adherents should:
>
> i) promote fair and equitable treatment for potential suppliers, by providing an adequate and timely degree of transparency in each phase of the public procurement cycle, while taking into account the legitimate needs for protection of trade secrets and proprietary information and other privacy concerns, as well as the need to avoid information that can be used by interested suppliers to distort competition in the procurement process. Additionally, suppliers should be required to provide appropriate transparency in subcontracting relationships.
>
> ii) allow free access, through an online portal, for all stakeholders, including potential domestic and foreign suppliers, civil society and the general public, to public procurement information, notably related to the public procurement system (e.g. institutional frameworks, laws and regulations), the specific procurements (e.g. procurement forecasts, calls for tender, award announcements) and the performance of the public procurement system (e.g. benchmarks, monitoring results). Published data should be meaningful for stakeholder uses.
>
> iii) ensure visibility of the flow of public funds, from the beginning of the budgeting process through the public procurement cycle, to *i)* let stakeholders understand government priorities and spending, and *ii)* allow policy makers to organise procurement strategically.
>
> *Source:* (OECD, 2015[12]).

Transparency is widely regarded as an effective tool for fighting corruption. According to OECD research, countries should implement internal control and regulatory oversight, supported by transparency and active participation by civil society in the public decision-making process (OECD, 2016[13]), to enable effective accountability. However, to be effective, transparency and accountability systems must be linked, and disclosing information should take account of the quality of what is disclosed as well as its quantity.

> **Box 2.6. Linking systems of accountability and transparency: *Subsidios al Campo* in Mexico**
>
> In 2008, a coalition between civil society organisations and interest groups launched an online platform called *Subsidios al Campo en México*, or Farm Subsidies in Mexico (*Subsidios*, www.subsidiosalcampo.org.mx). The coalition launched the website as an online tool to strengthen transparency by disclosing information and data on federal farm subsidies. The website also includes aggregated data on subsidies by state, municipality and region, as well as across years and types of programmes.
>
> The information is presented dynamically on the website, using graphics, figures and maps to aid comprehension and comparative analysis. According to the website, the initiative aimed to systematise information from different sources (state ministries, decentralised agencies, research centres and media). By various measures, *Subsidios* has been successful in increasing transparency, but underlying assumptions about the linkages and inter-reliance between transparency and accountability mechanisms and actors presented several issues. The assumptions included:
>
> - Public and accessible information would be used by civil society organisations and citizens to demand government action.
> - Key accountability actors involved in agricultural policy would be responsive to the demands of citizens, and use the information to improve oversight functions.
> - The executive branch, including the Ministry of Agriculture, would be equally responsive to the findings and recommendations of control entities, leading to policy reforms.
>
> In the case of *Subsidios*, the online portal was generally a success, but key users of the data did not have the incentive or capacity to use the information. Traditional pitfalls of online transparency policies also include barriers to information access and the resistance of government entities to public disclosure (Shkabatur, 2012[14]). Barriers to information access involve not only public disclosure of information (quantity), but also the manner in which it is disclosed (quality) and whether the public or accountability actors can analyse and understand the information.
>
> The assumptions in the case of *Subsidios* illustrate the important relationship between transparency initiatives and accountability mechanisms. Transparency systems rely on mechanisms for accountability to achieve certain outcomes, and vice versa. As illustrated by the assumptions in the case of *Subsidios*, actors within a system of accountability have responsibilities for transparency initiatives if they are to affect policy change.
>
> *Source:* (Cejudo, 2012[15]); (Shkabatur, 2012[14]); (Subsidios al Campo, 2017[16]).

SFP has recently led efforts to promote the anti-corruption agenda in Mexico. In March 2017, Mexico's federal government established an Alliance for Open Contracting (*Alianza para las contrataciones abiertas*) involving stakeholders from the public and private sectors, with the objective of adopting the Open Contracting Data Standard (OCDS) for all government procurement contracts at central and local levels (Coordinación de Estrategia Digital Nacional (National Digital Strategy Coordination), 2017[17]). The adoption of the OCDS is expected to directly impact the work done in

CompraNet. The OCDS facilitates the structured publication of data from all phases of the public procurement process: planning, tendering, awarding, contracting and implementation.

Although the Mexican government has agreed to implement the OCDS, the information currently published on CompraNet does not provide "shareable, reusable, machine readable data" as required by the OCDS. The current state of CompraNet data does not easily allow comprehensive analysis of procurement activities, given that:

- As tender responses are often submitted in hard copy, data is uploaded by scanning documents into PDF formats, which are not easily readable, making it challenging to extract data fields in a standardised fashion.
- Functionality for electronic signatures is not currently used, meaning that contracts cannot be entered into the system in open data format.
- The large number of open fields make it difficult to easily search and input data in a standardised way.
- Lack of compliance with naming conventions and agreed referencing standards reduce the quality and searchability of data in CompraNet. This also makes it difficult to link it with data or processes in other government systems.

In developing an approach to the implementation of the OCDS, consideration should be given to information that should not be made publicly available. In addition to data privacy requirements, there are limits to the effectiveness of full transparency on tender information. According to the OECD's Working Party on Competition, "full transparency of the procurement process and its outcome can promote collusion. Disclosing information such as the identity of the bidders and the terms and conditions of each bid allows competitors to detect deviations from a collusive agreement, punish those firms and better co-ordinate future tenders" (OECD, 2011[18]). Full transparency can also result in the sharing of commercially sensitive information, such as pricing models and profit margins implemented by businesses, which could discourage businesses from participating in public procurement opportunities. Commercially sensitive information can thus be captured by the system and made available to control entities, such as audit institutions, without being made publicly available in a way that encourages collusion.

Accountability can still be achieved in a somewhat constrained transparency environment, through enhanced systematisation or traceability of decisions through the procurement process. E-procurement can eliminate corruption opportunities from public procurement if it is designed to ensure that rules and procedures are standardised and consistent. This can restrict the existence of discretion in decision-making processes (Heggstad and Frøystad, 2011[19]). By including evaluation criteria and weightings in tender documents and establishing the evaluation criteria within the system in advance, tender responses can be evaluated against such criteria. This activity can be conducted without direct oversight from the public, using the functionality of the system to evaluate the tender against predefined criteria, whilst avoiding the publication of commercially sensitive information.

According to the findings from a global forum on corruption in public procurement hosted by the OECD's Competition Division, a number of other methods could be used to make collusion more difficult, while maintaining transparency and safeguarding the need to reduce the risk of corruption:

- Only information on the winning bid should be released, while information on the losing bids could be made available only to issuers of tenders and comptrollers, and not to competitors generally.
- Because of the potentially destabilising effect of nonidentifiable bidders on bid rigging, the procurement official might consider keeping the identities of the bidders undisclosed, perhaps referring only to bidder numbers and the number of bidders remaining in the bidding process.
- The timing of the disclosure of sensitive information (such as the losing bidders' identity and their bids) could be delayed to ease the effects of such disclosure on collusion (OECD, 2010[20]).

In order to satisfy the OCDS requirements, SFP and contracting authorities are currently spending significant resources on scanning and uploading procurement documents. This administrative work would not be required following a shift to the full use of the OCDS. According to the Open Contracting Partnership (OCP), the group responsible for developing the OCDS, several countries and cities have already benefited from the transition to the standard, as mentioned in the box below.

Box 2.7. Open Contracting Data Standard in Ukraine

After the Maidan revolution, civil society, the private sector and the government in Ukraine came together to make the provision of humanitarian resources more transparent. Based on this experience, civic activists and procurement experts formed a public-private partnership, the ProZorro initiative, to work on expanding this experience to make Ukraine's procurement system more publicly accessible.

The new system, based on the Open Contracting Data Standard, was launched in February 2015. It makes any document and information related to public procurement (including annual plans, tender notices and documentation, bids, decisions of evaluation committees and contracts) freely accessible online as open data. The results of the project have been impressive: in the first three months, USD 1.5 million in public funds was saved and competition increased from an average of two participating bidding companies per tender to three.

After the adoption of the new public procurement law in December 2015, and since it became mandatory on 1 April 2016, ProZorro was scaled up to include all procurement in Ukraine. The success of the project, all the more impressive considering the conflict in the country, was largely due to the collaboration between different stakeholders. For them, this project went far beyond open data as a principle. The implementation was results-oriented, not only in terms of numbers and savings but also in terms of transforming the business culture into something more beneficial for the country. Ukraine's project has been shared as a success with others in the field. ProZorro won the World Procurement Award in the Public Sector.

Source: (Open Contracting Partnership, 2017[21]).

The transition to the OCDS can be facilitated through use of guidance and tools provided by the OCP itself. According to its experiences of working with countries and cities to implement the OCDS, implementation should follow the steps below:

1. **Design your engagement and make a commitment:** identify the key goals to be achieved, engage with stakeholders and assemble a team with technology and policy skills;
2. **Map the readiness for open contracting in your country:** map data and documents to the OCDS to identify what data is required to meet user needs and what is missing.
3. **Build your Open Contracting Data Standard implementation:** create data releases by amending existing tools or using new ones in order to transform data and documents;
4. **Publish contracting data:** publish in line with a policy that dictates how information is kept up to date and how privacy and confidentiality are managed.
5. **Use information to monitor government contracts and fix problems:** build tools that make the data usable and leverage it to encourage accountability.
6. **Learn and innovate government contracting:** make adjustments to ensure a continuous improvement cycle.
7. **Show and share what you have learned with others:** document progress and monitor against original objectives (Open Contracting Partnership, 2017[22]).

Once the transition to the OCDS is made, tender submissions and contract details become much more traceable and auditable within the system. The transition will, however, require users and suppliers to be well trained, and the changes from hard-copy tender submissions and manual signatures to electronic documents must be carefully managed. In Chile, the transition from paper-based and "mixed" tender submissions to electronic tender documents required *Chile Compra* to provide incentives for suppliers and contracting authorities, for example:

- intensifying the number of audits on mixed and physical processes, while communicating the strategy clearly to contracting authorities
- using the system's Terms and Conditions of Use to establish a strict and demanding deadline for uploading paper-based tender files
- communicating statistics on the number of upload errors made by contracting authorities to the supplier community
- calculating the cost of the hours the contracting authority spent uploading documents and disseminating results to demonstrate efficiency gaps across the public sector.

By transitioning fully to the OCDS, the data in CompraNet will become much more usable and provide a solid platform for subsequent analysis. This will be used to enhance accountability, monitor compliance with procurement policy and improve decision making in relation to the impact of public procurement policy on contracting authorities, suppliers, and the wider economy. The continuous learning aspect of the OCDS implementation will be critical for ongoing improvements and requires constant feedback to be gathered from users. As functionality such as drop-downs and restricted options are implemented in order to avoid open fields, it will be necessary to ensure that users are still able to manage the system to input the necessary information.

Considering stakeholders' requirements can help SFP gather data that leads to insights

A number of stakeholder groups require information from CompraNet for a variety of reasons, for example in order to conduct trend analysis, investigate malpractice, formulate policy or undertake market analysis. All these actors play a role in the effective running of the Mexican public procurement system and rely on information in CompraNet to carry out their roles. A data management strategy for CompraNet should thus ensure that the information is comprehensive and accessible and that stakeholders can use it effectively.

Not all stakeholder groups have access to CompraNet, and those that do find it challenging to access the information they need. For example, the contracting authority *Instituto Mexicano del Seguro Social* (IMSS) has 544 000 workers and an audit team of 504, which constitutes less than 0.1% of the overall workforce. The organisation spends MXN 1 billion per day (USD 56.5 million). The majority of spending is centralised, with 93% carried out at the central level through contracts in CompraNet. Currently, the IMSS audit team is limited in its ability to use information in CompraNet to identify issues with procurement processes. If properly used, the data in CompraNet could be leveraged to enable audit teams at contracting authorities to conduct targeted, as opposed to random, audit investigations.

Box 2.8. Korea's Bid-Rigging Indicator Analysis System (BRIAS)

The Fair Trade Commission (FTC) in Korea works with public buying entities to identify cartel activity and potential cases of bid rigging in public procurement. This work is particularly relevant today, since a number of potential cases related to increased spending in response to the 2009 economic crisis have been identified. In 2009 and 2010, Korea launched a number of large public works projects in a limited period, and there are now claims that contractors colluded to divide up this work.

To identify cases of collusion, the FTC traditionally relied on voluntary reporting by cartel members seeking leniency, and on reports by competing suppliers. These remain the most reliable sources for identifying potential collusion. In 2006, the FTC developed the Bid-Rigging Indicator Analysis System (BRIAS) to supplement these methods of identification.

Drawing information directly from the Korean e-procurement system KONEPS, BRIAS analyses data elements including bidding price (as a ratio compared to reference price), the number of participants, and the competition method, and applies a formula that generates a potential bid-rigging score. If it is above a certain threshold, it suggests the need to collect more information on the contract action. Based on this information, an investigation is opened in cases where it is warranted.

BRIAS collects information from KONEPS on a daily basis, and each month, the system is run on data collected in the previous months. For goods and services, BRIAS is run on tenders above USD 423 800. For public works, the threshold is USD 4.2 million. As of 2012, BRIAS was run on 20 000 to 30 000 bids per year; of approximately 20 000 runs in 2012, the system generated 200 hits that warranted an additional look. This kind of automated system for detecting red flags in public procurement is a good practice that has been implemented successfully in other countries, such as Brazil.

Source: (OECD, 2016[7]).

Each of the stakeholder groups has different information needs, which must be understood before designing effective search and analysis tools and to ensure databases are appropriately structured. For example, auditors may require information aggregated by entity, with the possibility of drilling down to identify exceptions to open tender and to develop a targeted audit plan. This will enable Internal Control Bodies to ensure that contracting authorities follow a competitive process through CompraNet, except where there is a valid exception. Procurement operators need data to formulate market strategies, and policy makers need to be able to detect macro-patterns to identify opportunities for collaboration across government and to assess the impact of public procurement policy on the supply market.

According to the consultancy firm PricewaterhouseCoopers (PwC), e-procurement makes it possible to detect and prevent corruption in public procurement if data on tenders, bidders and contractors are collected and stored in a structured way and made accessible for investigation and analysis. For example, post-tender monitoring and analysis could identify evidence of corruption (e.g. number of contracts awarded to the same bidder, number of bidders, etc.); data mining could then be used to detect anomalies and to reveal potential cases of fraud or corruption (PwC; Ecorys, 2013[23]).

Table 2.1. Data needs of typical stakeholders

	Aggregated information requirements	Disaggregated information requirements
Contracting authorities	• Registered suppliers by category • Spending by category • Spending by supplier • P-card use	• Addressable spending • Savings realised vs. market rate • Payment times • Contract compliance by supplier • P-card use by employee
Audit institutions	• Number of direct awards and exceptions • Tender submission times	• Spent vs contract rate • Exception vs. supply market
Civil society	• Number of direct awards and exceptions by contracting authority • Average bid per tender	• Number of bids for specific procurements
Suppliers	• Opportunity by category • Contract award by supplier	• Contract award by supplier
Central purchasing bodies/policy makers	• Spending information by category Framework contract spending • Contracting authority spending information • Contract compliance by supplier • Contract award by SMEs/woman-owned businesses	• Framework contract compliance
Competition authorities	• Spending by supplier • Bid value trends • Bid win patterns	• Number of bids for specific procurements

Note: The spending requirements above are for illustrative purposes only and represent data that might ideally be available to stakeholders.
Source: Based on stakeholder interviews.

Not all the information above will be available in the system as it currently stands. According to a Deloitte survey of private sector chief procurement officers (CPOs), analytics is estimated to be the technology area that will have the largest impact on procurement in the next two years (65%), but limited data integration is the second-greatest barrier to the effective application of digital technologies (Deloitte, 2017[24]). In developing the CompraNet data management strategy, consideration should be given to how data needs to be collected and structured as systems are gradually integrated with CompraNet, to ensure that the needs of stakeholders are met in the future.

Given the diversity of stakeholders and their different needs, any user interface that is developed to enable access to data must be user-friendly, with training provided. According to a report on Business Intelligence (BI) strategies, the ease of use of the system is a key driver in the value that stakeholders can extract from data (Howson, 2010[25]). A survey of BI system users showed that, regardless of the simplicity of the BI interface, only a small portion (19%) say no formal training should be required, whereas in reality, 37% of respondents received no training at all. Twenty percent of survey respondents would like at least half a day of training, and nearly half (48%) would prefer one or two days or more of training. The study recommended that ease of use should be considered for various stakeholders and user groups, to develop:

- a BI solution that is easy to deploy and enhance
- BI content that is easy for "power users" to create, such as reports and dashboards
- dashboards and reports that are easy for typical users to interact with, explore and consume
- data presented in a way that makes it easy to draw insights once it is accessed.

However, a key consideration that precedes the implementation of a BI tool is that the data within the system be accurate, as BI tools require good data to generate meaningful insights.

Maintaining data integrity will take good governance in and outside CompraNet

The reliability of the data within CompraNet depends on information inputs being accurate, timely and complete. The Deloitte survey of CPOs identified quality of data as the greatest barrier to the effective application of digital technologies (49%) (Deloitte, 2017[24]). Some of this can be managed through system changes, such as adding checkpoints and requiring the input of complete and unchangeable information before procurement processes can progress to the next stage. However, some elements of data integrity require users to be trained, incentivised and/or compelled to include accurate and timely data.

According to a study on data governance in procurement and supply chain solutions at private organisations, in concert with Bravo Solutions, only 20% of the 70 procurement professionals that responded are currently implementing a "data governance" programme. The ranking of "data quality" priorities were: accuracy (58%), valid data (18%), complete data (11%), consistent data (11%), unique data (11%) and timely data (11%). The study indicates that these concerns represent a serious impediment to migrating to a digital strategy and to being able to use advanced analytical tools with a high level of confidence (Handfield, Yacura and Soundararajan, 2017[26]).

There are several steps throughout the procurement cycle in which, according to stakeholders, data in CompraNet suffers from one of the challenges mentioned above. For example, Mexico has developed its own catalogue system, the *Clasificador Único de las Contrataciones Públicas* (CUCOP), but it is not systematically used by procurement officials. Lack of enforcement in the use of common classifiers leads to inaccurate and unusable data in CompraNet. Procurement officials thus have greater difficulty in accessing information on past procurement processes, such as pricing information and quantities procured for each good and service. This affects users' ability to perform such tasks as developing needs assessments, or conducting market research or calls for tender opportunities. Information within the system also supports applications for tender exceptions. If this process does not draw on accurate information, exceptions may be granted without the requisite data.

The table below identifies challenges raised during discussions with stakeholders, and the types of tactics that may be identified in a data management strategy. It is important to note that not all data or security issues can be resolved through the use of technology. A data management strategy requires tactics that blend technology, process change, training, and culture development, among other things (Handfield, Yacura and Soundararajan, 2017[26]).

Table 2.2. Techniques for managing data integrity issues

Procurement phase	Data issue	Possible methods of resolution
Market research	Results not consistently uploaded	• System function – user unable to progress to next phase without completing and uploading market research
Supplier registry	Disqualified suppliers are not removed from the system	• Automatic removal of black-listed suppliers
Tender classification	Tenders are not correctly classified	• Align with international classification standards • Additional user guidance on how classification system should be used
Tender – general	Data is not available when linked to a user account for an individual who has left the organisation	• Enable super users within contracting authorities to reassign tenders to other staff members
Tender – general	Concerns that multiple users may be able to access single account	• Hold super users/system administrators within contracting authorities to account for managing users' rights, and checking usage within procurement teams
Tender – general	Inconsistent use of naming conventions	• Provide guidance on use of the system's naming conventions
Tender – general	Inconsistent use of reference numbers	• Introduce system functionality that provides each tender a unique reference number that links into other systems
Contracts and contract variations	Incomplete registry of contracts and contract variations	• Publish list of missing contracts to contracting authorities, to encourage compliance • Disable users that have not uploaded contracts from completed tenders • Use future connection with the financial system to disable payments for inaccurate unit prices without submission of appropriate contract variations to adjust unit price accordingly

Source: Based on stakeholder interviews.

Some data elements that stakeholders insist are important for understanding the full picture of public procurement activity in Mexico are not at present required to be uploaded to CompraNet and are therefore not included in the system. First, where contracting authorities request an exception to an open tender process, the reasons for exemption are not made public. Civil society groups indicate that contracting authorities often erroneously select restrictive procurement procedures that involve direct negotiation with a single supplier, which is usually supported by inaccurate market research indicating that no other viable suppliers exist. However, valid exceptions to open competition undoubtedly do exist, including in highly sensitive cases such as procuring goods or services related to national security. Where appropriate, mandating and facilitating the publication of this information in a public-friendly format would enable the validation of those requests (for example, by conducting objective market research to verify contracting authorities' claims), eventually leading to an increase in competition by ensuring that exceptions are more likely to be correctly applied. Operators of CompraNet indicated that where they did try to input information into the system, the platform was not suitable for loading information on noncompetitive procedures, and that system changes would be required to facilitate this addition.

Second, contracts between contracting authorities and other contracting authorities or state-owned entities (for example, universities), under what is known as an Article 1 exemption (*Article 1, 5th paragraph, LAASSP & Article 1, 4th paragraph, LOPSRM*), are not required (or allowed) to be entered into CompraNet. According to investigations by *Animal Político* and *Mexicanos Contra la Corrupción y la Impunidad* (MCCI), by using Article 1 exceptions, MXN 7 670 million in public contracts were awarded, through eight public universities, to 186 companies. However, 128 of the companies were not entitled to receive public resources, given that they did not have the infrastructure or legal standing to provide the services for which they were hired, or simply because they did not formally exist (Animal Politico, 2017[27]). Even in these cases, contracting authorities are still obliged to apply standard procurement principles dictated by Article 134 of the Constitution. Given that it is not made publicly available or loaded into any central repository, information related to this significant proportion of government expenditure is not easily accessible.

Under the existing legal framework, the two aforementioned categories of information are not required to be made publicly available. Any system changes to enable the publication of this information may thus need to be reinforced by formalising these processes in law.

The quality of insights that can be derived from CompraNet will affect the system's ability to increase accountability, advise public policy and generate value for public funds. However, the quality of insights is dependent on the quality and completeness of the data that is entered into the system. A data management strategy that is not restricted to the use of technology levers can mitigate several data integrity risks.

Using CompraNet to improve procurement practices, encourage competition and optimise value for public money

Existing help desk and training services can be improved and supplemented

Adherents to the OECD's Recommendation of the Council on Public Procurement should build a system geared towards the use of efficient and effective procurement processes and reducing administrative red tape and costs. In an e-procurement context, that involves providing support to users of the platform, to maximise the benefits of the system's functionality. Training and guidance, supported by fit-for-purpose help desk services that respond to both buyers and suppliers will improve users' interaction with the system.

The need to support users to make the most of technology developments in procurement is not limited to Mexico. According to the OECD survey on public procurement, 40% of countries reported low levels of knowledge and skills in the use of ICT (OECD, 2016[1]). This is seen by OECD countries as the second most significant barrier to the effective use of e-procurement systems by contracting authorities.

CompraNet is currently supported by a three-person in-house help desk team that deals with phone and email-based enquiries and problems. This service is supplemented by self-service resources such as user guides, videos and manuals. The service responds to enquiries about procurement processes, policy and legislation. On average since 2010, the help desk has received 3 000 user enquiries each month, 70% of which are processed, while 30% remain unresolved. The relatively small size of the help desk team may explain why it cannot satisfy all enquiries.

By contrast, the *Colombia Compra Eficiente* help desk is staffed by a team of 30, made up of 2 supervisors, 1 quality assurance role, 1 trainer and 26 agents. The service is available to users in three different channels. Table 2.3 shows how agents are measured according to the number of issues resolved, and how the average number of enquiries per agent compares with Mexico's.

Table 2.3. Average monthly help desk Statistics at *Colombia Compra Eficiente* (2017)

	Enquiries received	Enquiries resolved	Enquiries per agent (monthly average)	Mexico enquiries per agent (monthly average) (1 January-2 October 2017)
Calls	8 911	6 744 (76%)	343	478
Chat	13 568	9 358 (69%)	522	N/A
Email	2 054	2 054 (100%)	79	423
Total	24 533	18 156 (74%)	944	443

Source: Data provided courtesy of *Colombia Compra Eficiente* and SFP.

The number of enquiries per agent between Colombia and Mexico is currently comparable. However, once awareness and use of CompraNet increases, and allowing for increases that will occur with system changes, the number of enquiries per agent in Mexico is likely to increase. The average number of user enquiries in Colombia is eight times higher than Mexico's. Similarly, the average number of enquiries per month in Chile (20 000) is nearly seven times greater than the monthly average in Mexico, implying that CompraNet users are not engaging with support services at the rate they do in other countries. This could either be attributed to a lack of awareness of the existence of support services, or suggest that CompraNet is a stable system well-understood by its users.

Exploring with non-users of support services their reasons for not engaging with the help desk sheds some light on user perception, as does engaging users in perception or feedback surveys. Efforts should be considered to measure user perception of the help desk service to ensure the service is customer-oriented and user-friendly. User satisfaction surveys can also measure changes in user perception over time.

The process of anticipating and planning for the effects of a significant business change on policies, behaviour, systems and processes is known as "change management". Following a significant change to the system (many of which are anticipated as the system Roadmap is implemented), the number of user enquiries is likely to increase significantly. The plan to manage changes to the system should acknowledge the likelihood of a spike in user enquiries. As demands on help-desk services increase, attention should also be paid to the changes that will be required in guidelines and training services. Communicating to users how the system should be used for conducting each step of the procurement cycle (for example needs assessments, market research or identifying qualifications and award criteria) will be key to the success of the improvements.

> **Box 2.9. Stakeholder training and e-procurement support in Colombia**
>
> In its work, *Colombia Compra Eficiente* emphasises the importance of engaging with stakeholders by giving them useful, relevant information. Its help desk for all stakeholders offers manuals and videos on using the electronic systems, and it also issues manuals and guides explaining how the procurement system works. *Colombia Compra Eficiente* also publishes a regular bulletin for interested stakeholders highlighting ongoing efforts and improvements. SECOP II, the second phase of Colombia's electronic procurement rollout, also provides opportunities to continue and expand stakeholder engagement.
>
> Government purchasing entities, suppliers and potential suppliers, control authorities, the media and NGOs and the general public all have a high degree of interest in receiving relevant information from the public procurement system. Government entities, suppliers and industry stakeholder groups who were interviewed expressed a strong interest in the reduction of effort that will result from the digitalisation of processes; the main concern was that the new system be adopted as soon as possible. Many also said they believed that the move to SECOP II and more clearly defined electronic processes will reduce the barriers facing potential new entrants in their first encounters with the public procurement process.
>
> Journalists are also heavy users of public procurement information provided by SECOP II. This group expressed surprise and satisfaction in interviews at the amount of information *Colombia Compra Eficiente* makes available, and also with the availability of staff to address questions about whether or not data was available. This group, like other stakeholders, expressed interest in the benefits likely to be realised in the transition to SECOP II. They anticipated that the new system was likely to result in higher quality data and better interconnection with other data sources. The timeliness of available information was cited as a critical concern for the stakeholders interviewed.
>
> Source: (OECD, 2016[11]).

Preparing users for changes to the system should also involve efforts to improve and expand system training both for suppliers and contracting authorities. For procurement officials and suppliers now using CompraNet, SFP has developed face-to-face training programmes, as well as online courses for self-training. Around 9 000 procurement officials had face-to-face training in the use of CompraNet between 2011 and 2017. However, information gathered during the OECD fact-finding mission suggests that many enquiries to CompraNet's help desk reveal a lack of knowledge of the system's processes and norms. Improving and supplementing ongoing system training opportunities for procurement officials is expected to reduce the reliance on the help desk for support and ensure that the system is being used as an effective tool for procurement. Building the capacity of the procurement workforce sustainably is a long-term effort, and strategies are needed to tackle both immediate and long-term issues.

> **Box 2.10. OECD's Recommendation of the Council on Public Procurement – principle on capacity**
>
> IX. RECOMMENDS that Adherents develop a procurement workforce with the capacity to continually deliver value for money efficiently and effectively.
>
> To this end, Adherents should:
>
> i) ensure that procurement officials meet high professional standards for knowledge, practical implementation and integrity by providing a dedicated and regularly updated set of tools, for example, sufficient staff in terms of numbers and skills, recognition of public procurement as a specific profession, certification and regular trainings, integrity standards for public procurement officials and the existence of a unit or team analysing public procurement information and monitoring the performance of the public procurement system.
>
> ii) provide attractive, competitive and merit-based career options for procurement officials, through the provision of clear means of advancement, protection from political interference in the procurement process and the promotion of national and international good practices in career development to enhance the performance of the procurement workforce.
>
> iii) promote collaborative approaches with knowledge centres such as universities, think tanks or policy centres, to improve skills and competences of the procurement workforce. The expertise and pedagogical experience of knowledge centres should be enlisted as a valuable means of expanding procurement knowledge and upholding a two-way channel between theory and practice, capable of boosting application of innovation to public procurement systems.
>
> *Source:* (OECD, 2015[12]).

Raising awareness of the system and building suppliers' capabilities to use it

Using CompraNet to increase value for public funds will mean engaging the business community. To increase supplier participation in public procurement, and to increase competition, barriers reducing supplier participation must be removed, particularly in the case of small and medium-sized enterprises (SMEs). According to the OECD survey on public procurement, the barriers for businesses in using e-procurement differ from those faced by contracting authorities. Barriers for businesses are more diverse and include limitations in their knowledge and skills in using ICT, difficulties in interacting with the system and understanding or applying the necessary procedures.

Figure 2.7. Challenges for businesses in effectively using e-procurement systems

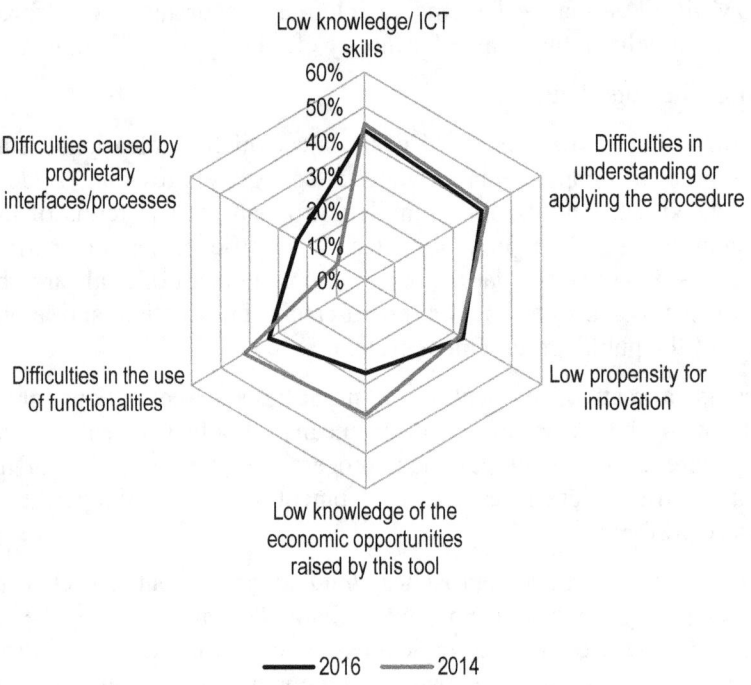

Source: (OECD, 2016[1]).

On average, 4.3 bid proposals were received for each open tender conducted in CompraNet from 2010 to date. SFP intends to increase this number in order to demonstrate the inclusiveness and competitiveness of public procurement in Mexico. Businesses that are not participating in public procurement opportunities can be divided into two groups: those that have access to the system and do not participate in public tenders, and those that do not have access to or are not aware of CompraNet.

> **Box 2.11. OECD's Recommendation of the Council on Public Procurement – principle on access**
>
> IV. RECOMMENDS that Adherents facilitate access to procurement opportunities for potential competitors of all sizes.
>
> To this end, Adherents should:
>
> ii) Deliver clear and integrated tender documentation, standardised where possible and proportionate to the need, to ensure that:
>
> 1) specific tender opportunities are designed so as to encourage broad participation from potential competitors, including new entrants and small and medium enterprises. This requires providing clear guidance to inform buyers expectations (including specifications and contract as well as payment terms) and binding information about evaluation and award criteria and their weights (whether they are focused specifically on price, include elements of price/quality ratio or support secondary policy objectives); and
>
> 2) the extent and complexity of information required in tender documentation and the time allotted for suppliers to respond is proportionate to the size and complexity of the procurement, taking into account any exigent circumstances such as emergency procurement.
>
> Source: (OECD, 2015[12]).

During the interviews, several reasons were suggested for the lack of participation by suppliers already registered in CompraNet. One reason was their inability to act on notifications of tender opportunities. It is not clear how effective the system's alert system is in letting suppliers know of tender opportunities in their field of interest. Some stakeholders suggested that many businesses request notifications in a broad range of categories, including some outside the industry in which they operate, and that the sheer volume of notifications is too great for businesses to identify and act on genuine opportunities. This suggests that suppliers registered in CompraNet could benefit from ongoing training on how to use the system effectively, and training to enhance understanding of how to be successful in responding to government tenders. The issue may also be attributed to the application of CUCOP, a bespoke, Mexican-developed system for classifying goods and services. By transitioning to a more universally recognised standard, SFP may be able to attract international suppliers while familiarising Mexican businesses with a system that they will need to use to export to other countries.

Since 2012, more than 14 000 suppliers have received face-to-face training. However, considering the total amount of suppliers registered in CompraNet (over 215 000 as of 2017, with over 3 000 new users registering each month), these training efforts should be enhanced, for example by educating suppliers on the relevant aspects of the Mexican legal system related to public procurement. The use of online training and the efforts to raise awareness about CompraNet can help educate suppliers outside major urban centres.

According to SFP, as of March 2017, 78% of contracts had been awarded to SMEs, representing 53.1% of the total contract value (a total of MXN 2 893 762 million since 2010). Of more than 5 million registered businesses in Mexico, over 70% are not registered in CompraNet. Around 1 million businesses in Mexico are informal, volatile and may not be a part of the government tax system, still leaving a pool of over 3 million businesses that could be encouraged to participate in public procurement. Engaging these suppliers, many of whom are likely to be SMEs, will mean eliminating barriers to participation, to ensure that CompraNet can be reached by suppliers of all sizes all over the country. The OECD public procurement survey identified a number of approaches used by member countries to encourage the participation of SMEs in public procurement (OECD, 2016[1]).

Figure 2.8. Approaches in place in OECD countries supporting the development of SMEs

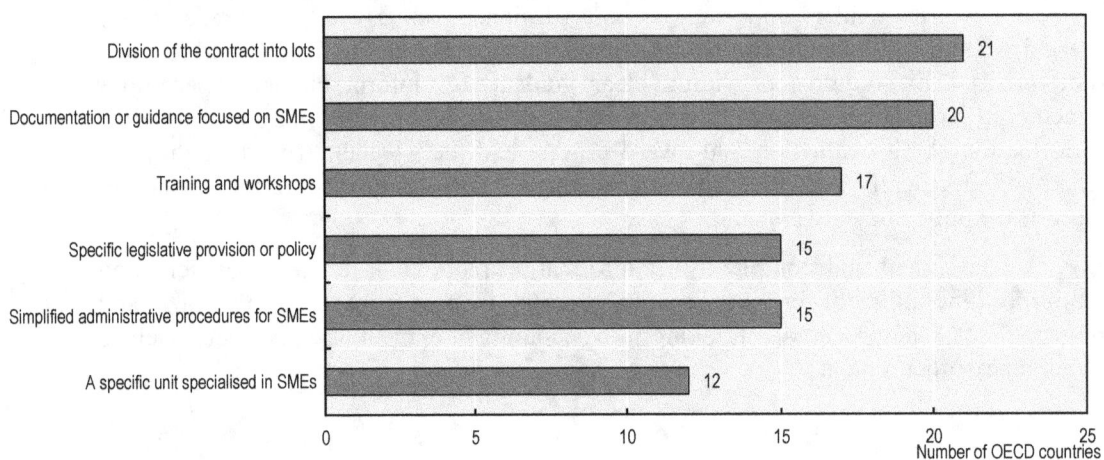

Source: (OECD, 2016[1]).

Other mechanisms for improving participation (and for enhancing suppliers' perceptions of public procurement processes as open and fair) include making sure that suppliers are provided with adequate feedback channels and complaint mechanisms where there are issues with a procurement process. The public procurement complaints process is currently located outside CompraNet, as part of a channel for collecting general complaints on the conduct of public officials. There are no specific instructions for filing complaints related to public procurement on the SFP website, and fields on the complaint form do not provide specific options or drop-downs on public procurement. Also, complainants are asked to indicate under which federal law they wish to complain, which requires businesses to have an advanced understanding of public procurement law.

Based on the complaints filed on that website, SFP holds a database of complaints directed against public officials. Of a total of 104 000 complaints, only 2% are related to public procurement. The low numbers could reflect the lack of clarity around the complaints process, or a culture averse to filing complaints. This is reinforced by the fact that Mexico did not launch any investigations or convictions involving foreign bribery between 2009 and 2014 (Bolongaita, 2017[28]). If CompraNet's role in allowing for acts of whistle-blowing is increased, corruption may be more easily identified and investigations initiated more frequently. The lack of clarity around the process can be resolved as part of supplier outreach and training, and by including instructions on how to submit complaints in relation to public procurement as part of future iterations of the CompraNet system. However, major cultural changes take time, and will be assisted by the government's openness to improving public procurement processes in response to suppliers' feedback.

> **Box 2.12. A whistle-blower hotline in Austria**
>
> In March 2013, Austria's Ministry of Justice set up a whistle-blower hotline on the home page of the Public Prosecutor's Office against Corruption and White-Collar Crime. As of September 2013, approximately 590 notifications were submitted through the platform. Only 53 of those notifications were not relevant.
>
> The Federal Ministry of Justice's whistle-blowing website enables investigators from the Public Prosecutor's Office against Corruption and White-Collar Crime (*Zentrale Staatsanwaltschaft zur Verfolgung von Wirtschaftsstrafsachen und Korruption*, WKStA) to get in direct contact with whistle-blowers to ensure their anonymity. In that event, the whistle-blower is entitled to decide whether he/she would like to remain anonymous or to identify him/herself to the investigators.
>
> *Source:* (OECD, 2016[11]).

Increasing competition in public procurement activity, and ultimately achieving improvements in value for money, requires a commitment to using the e-procurement system to better engage suppliers. This means building the capabilities of suppliers already registered on CompraNet, and among SMEs, raising awareness of CompraNet and its role in public procurement processes.

Standardising procurement documentation could reduce the cost of tendering and increase competition

For businesses, participating in public tenders can be costly and complex in an environment where each contracting authority uses different documentation and has different requirements for each tender. By standardising procurement practices in Mexico, using both system-centric and non-system-centric initiatives, transaction costs for suppliers will be reduced and suppliers will be more likely to participate in government tenders.

Central Purchasing Bodies (CPBs) across the OECD membership utilise a range of models to introduce procurement reform. Mexico's current system uses a decentralised approach (similar to that in Japan and Russia), leaving the majority of direct procurement to each contracting authority. The role of a CPB in this model is typically to encourage improvements in procurement practices, often by identifying opportunities to drive standardisation and collaboration between contracting authorities. Procurement reform is often initiated to realise cost savings and to improve a landscape where each agency has established its own procedures and processes. A proliferation of heterogeneous procurement procedures increases transaction costs, and inhibits supplier participation and competition.

The perspective of stakeholders in Mexico is that each contracting authority still uses its own form of procurement documentation and each has different requirements for suppliers. This drives up the cost for suppliers of participating in government procurement, in particular restricting the ability of organisations without significant resources (such as SMEs) to respond to tenders. Having standardised information requirements for the different documentation used in procurement processes is beneficial for all users. This can be achieved either by publishing new standardised documents or by enforcing a standardised order and arrangement of the information requirements included in each type of document (allowing entities to define their own wording for documents). Homogenising documentation and information requirements will create more efficiency for suppliers and government users. This process should be undertaken in advance of the introduction of open data standards, so that new document formats can use common fields that will allow data to be more easily extracted and analysed. In this sense, interoperability with other systems can be more easily achieved, allowing for automatic extraction of information and preliminary filling of response fields.

Document templates can be developed for different steps of the procurement process to ensure broad standardisation (e.g. model documents for invitations, tender documents and contracts). Commoditised goods and services are often a target for standardisation activities in public procurement, given the lack of unique and customised specifications. Developing a common approach and common specifications for the purchase of these types of goods across government, including in areas such as sustainability requirements, could improve the engagement between government and the suppliers of goods and services that are commonly used by the majority of contracting authorities. Other practices can help drive standardisation across a decentralised system, for example detailing the procedures that can be used to determine a bidder's eligibility and ability to perform a specific contract, and standardising time limits to make sure suppliers have ample time to identify and respond to procurement opportunities.

> **Box 2.13. Government Model Contracts in New Zealand**
>
> The New Zealand Ministry of Business, Innovation and Employment (MBIE) developed a set of standard contract terms and conditions for routine government purchases. These conditions are called government model contracts (GMCs).
>
> The development and implementation of GMCs is part of the Government Procurement Reform Programme and was mandated by a Cabinet Directive requiring MBIE to "create a standard, simple, plain English set of conditions of contract for common goods and services to be used by all Public Service Departments and State Services."
>
> The GMCs are aimed at low-value, low-risk common goods and services. They have been designed as the default government contract. It is up to each agency using the GMCs to determine what constitutes low-value, low-risk common goods and services. This definition is subjective and will depend on the size of the agency and the scale and complexity of its procurement function.
>
> Through the use of GMCs across the Public Service and State Services, government aims to:
>
> - provide simple, plain English contracts that are easy to use for both agencies and suppliers
> - provide a fairer balance of risk between buyer and supplier
> - standardise the treatment of legal risk in low-value, low-risk contracts
> - reduce the need for negotiations and legal advice in routine purchases
> - promote consistent practices across government
> - promote process efficiencies in high-volume, low-value transactional contracting
> - make it easier to do business with government
> - support improved procurement practice and align with international best practice.
>
> The results have been an overall increase in suppliers' satisfaction with government procurement practices recorded as part of the New Zealand Annual Business Survey.
>
> *Source:* (OECD, 2016$_{[11]}$).

Modifications can be made to CompraNet to further standardise procurement practices for the benefit of suppliers. For example, tools such as pre-qualification functionality can be used to streamline the procurement process for suppliers. Such tools can retain, for each supplier, information such as bank guarantees, insurance certificates, professional qualifications and other documentation that suppliers must provide as part of each tender process. This would prevent suppliers from having to produce the same documents repeatedly. It would be possible to expand a pre-qualification tool to include requirements relevant to certain industries, such as engineering qualifications or association memberships, although this would require contracting authorities to agree on standard requirements. Adapting the current Supplier Registry (*Registro Único de Proveedores y Contratistas*, RUPC) to meet this need is an option that could be explored.

The application of such tactics to standardise tender processes and documentation can lower entry barriers for businesses, and help in the monitoring and analysis of procurement activity. Such changes offer an opportunity for further improvements as e-procurement becomes a fully integrated end-to-end system collecting procurement data in an open and extractable format.

Note

[2] The OECD's Compendium of Good Practices for Integrity in Public Procurement has, since 2009, called for social witnesses to participate in all stages of public tendering procedures above certain monetary thresholds, as a way of promoting public scrutiny. As of 2017, the thresholds were MXN 400.2 million (approximately EUR 18.6 million) for goods, leasing and services, and MXN 800.4 million (approximately EUR 37.2 million) for public works and related services.

"Social witnesses" are nongovernmental organisations and individuals selected by the Ministry of Public Administration (SFP). SFP notes that "the monitoring of the most relevant procurement processes of the federal government through social witnesses has had an impact in improving procurement procedures by virtue of their contributions and experience, to the point that they have become a strategic element for ensuring the transparency and credibility of the procurement system" (OECD, 2015[29]).

References

Animal Politico (2017), *La Estafa Maestra: Graduados en desaparecer dinero público*, http://www.animalpolitico.com/estafa-maestra/ (accessed on 08 September 2017). [27]

Asian Development Bank (2013), *e-Government Procurement Handbook*, https://www.adb.org/sites/default/files/institutional-document/34064/files/e-government-procurement-handbook.pdf (accessed on 20 November 2017). [2]

Bolongaita, E. (2017), *Mandate without means: Strengthening the OECD Anti-Bribery Convention*, Carnegie Mellon University, Australia, https://www.oecd.org/cleangovbiz/Integrity-Forum-2017-Bolongaita-oecd-anti-bribery-convention.pdf (accessed on 18 September 2017). [28]

Cejudo, G. (2012), *Evidence for Change: The Case of Subsidios al Campo in Mexico*, https://www.internationalbudget.org/wp-content/uploads/LP-case-study-Fundar.pdf (accessed on 20 November 2017). [15]

Coordinación de Estrategia Digital Nacional (National Digital Strategy Coordination) (2017), *Datos abiertos en la agenda anticorrupción*, https://datos.gob.mx/blog/datos-abiertos-en-la-agenda-anticorrupcion?category=proyectos&tag=%20finanzas-y-contrataciones (accessed on 22 November 2017). [17]

Deloitte (2017), "Growth: the cost and digital imperative The Deloitte Global Chief Procurement Officer Survey 2017", http://www.deloitte.co.uk/cposurvey2017 (accessed on 08 September 2017). [24]

EBRD; UNCITRAL (2015), *Are you ready for eProcurement?*, European Bank for Reconstruction and Development; United Nations Commission on International Trade Law, https://www.ppi-ebrd-uncitral.com/index.php/en/component/content/article/427-ebrd-is-launching-a-guide-to-eprocurement-reform-are-you-ready-for-eprocurement (accessed on 14 September 2017). [3]

El Financiero (2017), *Gobierno prepara programa para encontrar 'fantasmas' en licitaciones*, http://www.elfinanciero.com.mx/economia/gobierno-prepara-programa-para-encontrar-fantasmas-en-licitaciones.html (accessed on 08 September 2017). [10]

Handfield, R., J. Yacura and B. Soundararajan (2017), "How Governance of Data and Technology Drive the Intelligence Spectrum in Supply Chain and Procurement", https://cdn2.hubspot.net/hubfs/514030/1_Amer_BravoSolution/AMER_2017/2017_Whitepapers/15.%20DataGovernanceReport/2017_WP_DataGovernanceProcurement_EN_US.pdf (accessed on 08 September 2017). [26]

Heggstad, K. and M. Frøystad (2011), *The basics of integrity in procurement*, http://www.u4.no/publications/the-basics-of-integrity-in-procurement (accessed on 13 September 2017). [19]

Howson, C. (2010), *Ease of Use and Interface Appeal in Business Intelligence Tools*, March 22, http://www.beyeresearch.com/study/13006 (accessed on 07 September 2017). [25]

OECD (2010), "Collusion and Corruption in Public Procurement", https://www.oecd.org/competition/cartels/46235884.pdf (accessed on 18 September 2017). [20]

OECD (2011), "Competition and Procurement", http://www.oecd.org/daf/competition/sectors/48315205.pdf (accessed on 13 September 2017). [18]

OECD (2011), *E-procurement, Brief 17*, SIGMA-OECD. [4]

OECD (2014), "Recommendation of the Council on Digital Government Strategies", http://www.oecd.org/gov/digital-government/Recommendation-digital-government-strategies.pdf (accessed on 14 September 2017). [9]

OECD (2015), "Effective Delivery of Large Infrastructure Projects: The Case of the New International Airport for Mexico City". [8]

OECD (2015), "OECD Recommendation of the Council on Public Procurement", https://www.oecd.org/gov/ethics/OECD-Recommendation-on-Public-Procurement.pdf (accessed on 14 September 2017). [12]

OECD (2015), "Compendium of Good Practices for Integrity in Public Procurement: Meeting of the Leading Practitioners in Procurement". [29]

OECD (2016), *2016 OECD Survey on Public Procurement*. [1]

OECD (2016), "The Korean Public Procurement Service Innovating for Effectiveness", http://www.oecd-ilibrary.org/docserver/download/4215251e.pdf?expires=1505401890&id=id&accname=ocid84004878&checksum=335B2E0D525A850CD687D7FC819A97D7 (accessed on 14 September 2017). [7]

OECD (2016), "Towards Efficient Public Procurement in Colombia: Making the Difference", http://dx.doi.org/10.1787/9789264252103-en. [11]

OECD (2016), "Putting an End to Corruption", Vol. 3/33, https://www.oecd.org/corruption/putting-an-end-to-corruption.pdf (accessed on 26 September 2017), pp. 23-45. [13]

OECD (2017), "Development and implementation of a national e-procurement strategy for the Slovak Republic", http://www.oecd.org/governance/procurement/toolbox/search/slovakia-e-procurement-strategy.pdf (accessed on 18 September 2017). [5]

Open Contracting Partnership (2017), *Open Contracting Partnership Showcase Projects - Ukraine*, https://www.open-contracting.org/why-open-contracting/showcase-projects/ukraine/ (accessed on 07 September 2017). [21]

Open Contracting Partnership (2017), *The Open Contracting Journey: Step-by-Step*, https://www.open-contracting.org/wp-content/uploads/2017/01/7-steps-guidance.pdf (accessed on 07 September 2017). [22]

PwC; Ecorys (2013), "Identifying and Reducing Corruption in Public Procurement in the EU", https://ec.europa.eu/anti-fraud/sites/antifraud/files/docs/body/identifying_reducing_corruption_in_public_procurement_en.pdf (accessed on 13 September 2017). [23]

Shkabatur, J. (2012), "Transparency with(out) accountability: Open government in the United States", *Yale Law & Policy Review*, Vol. 31/1, http://www.jstor.org/stable/23735771, pp. 79-140. [14]

Subsidios al Campo (2017), *About this project*, http://subsidiosalcampo.org.mx/acerca-de/sobre-este-proyecto/. [16]

United Nations (2006), *UN Procurement Practitioner's Handbook*, https://www.ungm.org/Areas/Public/pph/ch04s02.html (accessed on 14 September 2017). [6]

Chapter 3. A multi-phase roadmap for upgrading CompraNet from compliance to integration

The Roadmap developed by the OECD is the product of the recommendations of the Subgroups under the guidance of the Ministry of Public Administration (Secretaría de la Función Pública, SFP), co-ordinated and streamlined by the OECD based on international best practices. Additional guidance is provided on how best to implement the Roadmap, given the many considerations surrounding the execution of a programme of this complexity. This chapter outlines the course of action proposed by the Roadmap and evaluates each action in the light of the other dimensions affected, including technological, legal, procedural and governance considerations. This reinforces the need to apply a holistic approach to implementation that takes into account the implications of each change in the e-procurement system.

A comprehensive programme for the CompraNet Roadmap

A multi-phase rollout will set up building blocks for subsequent phases

A phased approach to implementation has generally been advocated by the OECD in other e-procurement implementation projects. This is common in large, transformative projects, as it allows for closer monitoring and control. It also reduces the impact of change on users of the system and other stakeholders, and allows for modifications in plans and approach in response to developments in the political environment or technology (OECD, 2017[1]).

Guidance provided by many development banks on implementing national e-procurement systems suggests that a gradual approach to e-procurement reform is advisable, particularly in countries that have developed their foundations through steady advances in the definition of e-government procurement policies, successive legal reforms and, in general, the use of cumulative processes (Procurement Harmonization Project of the Asian Development Bank, 2004[2]). This study proposed a gradual approach that would divide implementation into four phases, namely:

1. Preparation: This is a definitive phase for the success of e-government procurement. Three basic prerequisites for start-up are in play: what (vision), who (institutional framework and leadership), and how (action plan).
2. Tendering: The objective of this phase is to conduct tendering processes within shorter time frames, at a lower cost for both suppliers and the government, with transparency, and with a high impact on development.
3. Contract management: This phase entails developing the capacity to perform on line, and therefore at lower cost, with high transparency, contract management activities such as monitoring of partial and final delivery of goods, services and works, intermediate and final payment management, and contract variations or adjustments.
4. Purchasing: The objective of this phase is to develop a directly transactional system. Suppliers may offer their goods and services, allowing public entities to select the best option among them on line, manage supply and receipt, update inventories accordingly, and request and process payment.

The Roadmap for CompraNet was developed with this in mind, taking into account the specific context of Mexico, the current state of the CompraNet system and the lessons learned in other OECD reviews of Mexico's institutions. The improvements are divided into areas corresponding to the remit of the Subgroups. However, some recommendations have been amended or combined with others to develop a cohesive Roadmap for the system.

- *Phase 1 – Compliance-Driven System:* the first phase will run to November 2018, which does not leave sufficient time to introduce significant operational changes. Instead, the focus of the first phase is on increasing human compliance with the system (i.e. making sure that officials upload accurate, complete and timely information and running a permanent audit programme on the information uploaded). It will also focus on marketing the system to suppliers, and developing operational changes that resolve some of the system's most pressing challenges, that is, reducing the opportunities for corruption (i.e. providing data to focus audits on procurement, and setting up mechanisms to make it possible for whistle-blowers to come forward if necessary).

- *Phase 2 – Open Data Friendly System:* the second phase, which will cover a three-year period from the end of Phase 1 (2018-2020) will involve a transition to an open data system, changing the way in which data is entered into the system. The goal is to safeguard the integrity of the information in the system, and allow stakeholders to use the data more easily.
- *Phase 3 – Fully Integrated Transactional System:* the third phase, starting at the end of Phase 2 (2020-2027), will make the transition to a fully transactional system. It will link with contracting authority platforms and allow oversight of the full procurement cycle.

Multiple levers can be used to implement changes to CompraNet and the wider procurement system

Changing how procurement professionals operate, particularly when using an e-procurement system, does not necessarily require legislative reform. Many different levers can be employed, each with different levels of flexibility. Many operational changes within the system may be instituted without the need for new legislation.

Of the levers available to Public Procurement Authorities or Central Purchasing Bodies (CPBs) to drive procurement reform, legislation is the least flexible option, although it is typically used to implement it. A report by the United Kingdom's National Audit Office says regulation "can also create costs for businesses, the third and the public sectors. It can, if overused, poorly designed or implemented, stifle competitiveness and growth" (National Audit Office, 2014[3]). Where regulations are used, tools such as regulatory impact analysis (RIA) and consultation can be used to measure the likely benefits, costs and effects of new regulation and examine changes to existing ones (OECD, 2005[4]).

Figure 3.1. Procurement levers by level of flexibility

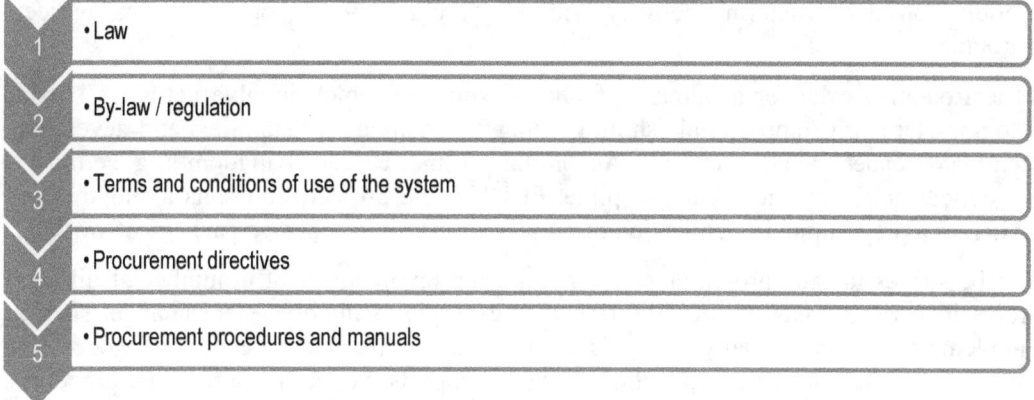

Source: Courtesy of G. Burr; *Chile Compra*.

Furthermore, in addition to the impact analysis conducted in advance of legislation, the evaluation of existing laws and regulations through *ex post* impact analysis is necessary to ensure that they are effective and efficient. The overall burden of complying with regulations tends to increase over time, complicating the daily life of citizens and impeding the efficient operation of business. *Ex post* evaluation can be the final stage of the regulatory policy cycle, evaluating the extent to which regulations meet the goals they were designed to achieve. It can also be the initial point for understanding the impact, shortcomings and advantages of a policy or regulation, and provide feedback for the design of new regulations. This process could be a beneficial exercise in advance of the forthcoming review of Mexican procurement legislation (OECD, 2014[5]).

Weighing the technology purchasing option that offers the best long-term solution

It is important to note that the Roadmap does not seek to determine at what point (or whether) CompraNet should be migrated to a new platform, and whether the platform should be developed in house, developed externally or bought as an "off-the-shelf" system. This decision will require an analysis of the cost of each option and the capacity for upgrading the current platform in line with the recommendations in the Roadmap.

According to Gartner's Magic Quadrant eSourcing report of 2015, which evaluates supplier trends in the e-procurement market, 81% of organisations providing input to the report deploy multitenant Software as a Service (SaaS) (a single instance of software running on a server and serving multiple parties). Fourteen percent use a system stored within a private cloud and the remaining 5% have their own, stand-alone installation on the premises (Gartner, 2015[6]). This demonstrates the extent to which SaaS is the most prevalent form of application for organisations selecting e-procurement applications.

Each form has different advantages and disadvantages, depending on the context and requirements of the organisation. A thorough cost/benefit analysis should consider all possible deployment options.

A diverse programme of work will require individuals with specialised skills

To date, the CompraNet project has demonstrated a commitment to establishing effective governance involving multiple stakeholders. This approach should be continued, to ensure that the project has suitable direction and oversight. However, given the multitude of changes (in terms of behaviour, culture, processes, roles, etc.) that a new or heavily amended system would introduce, the team set up to deliver the CompraNet Roadmap should consider structuring delivery within a "programme" as opposed to a "project" structure.

The Roadmap calls for a number of phases, some of which involve activities outside CompraNet (for example establishing training programmes for suppliers and developing template tender documentation). According to the United Kingdom's government-designed project management discipline, PRINCE2, a project represents a single effort, whereas a programme is a collection of projects that form a cohesive package of work.

To be successful, the programme will require the involvement of a number of different roles in various areas of specialisation. For example, a major system change, such as implementing a universally recognised standard for the classification of goods and services, is likely to have implications for legal aspects, human resources and processes. This must be managed carefully by individuals with the requisite expertise, including experts in managing change within organisations.

A number of activities will require ongoing delivery, both during and after the programme. For example, initiatives to develop capacity will need to be continuously delivered and modified, depending on the state of the system. With each change to the system or processes, system handbooks, guidance and training modules will need to be updated. Given the importance of the capability of users in working with the system, an ongoing system training programme is a worthwhile investment.

3. A MULTI-PHASE ROADMAP FOR UPGRADING COMPRANET FROM COMPLIANCE TO INTEGRATION | 77

Figure 3.2. CompraNet Roadmap

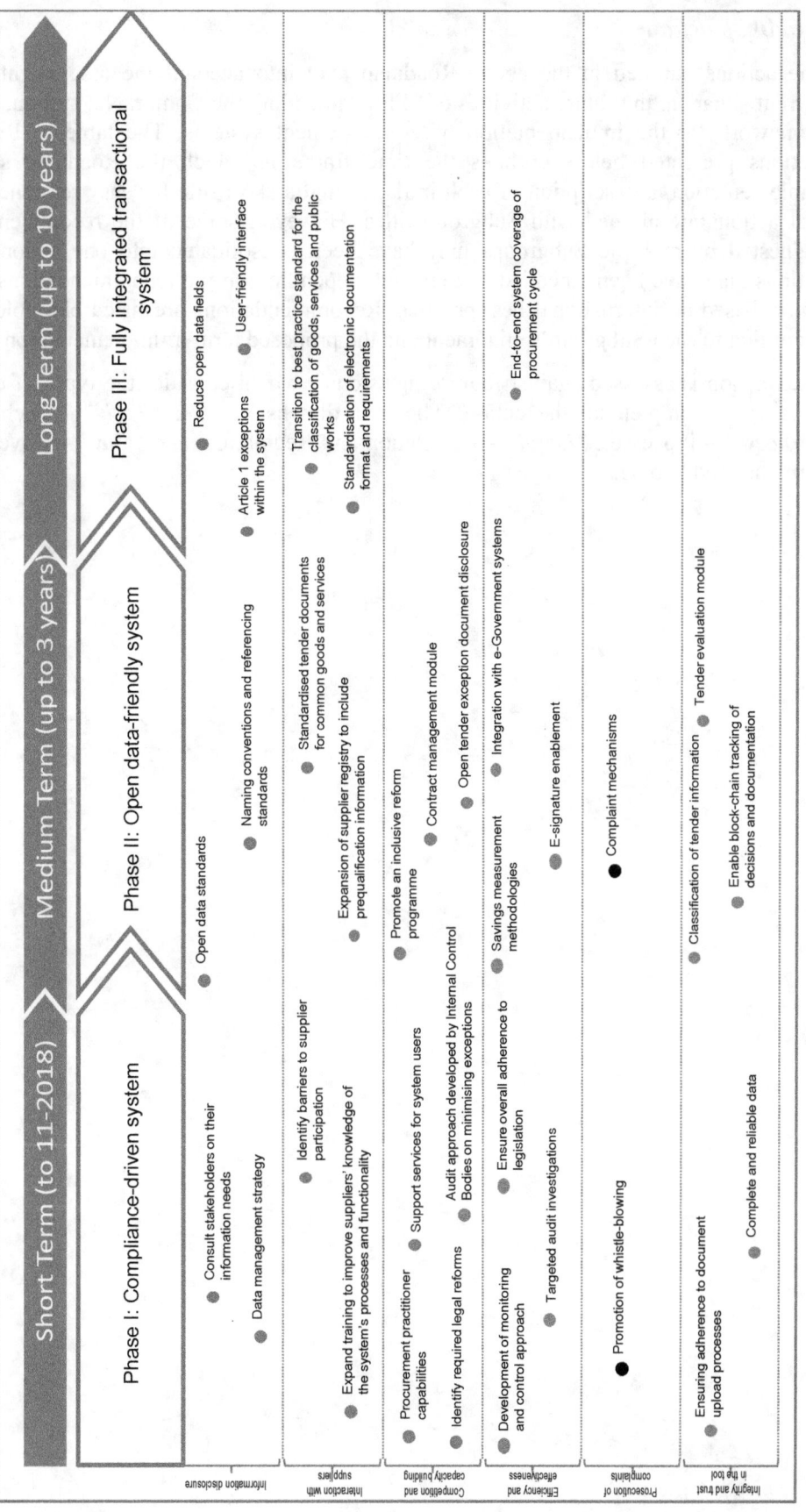

MEXICO'S E-PROCUREMENT SYSTEM: REDESIGNING COMPRANET THROUGH STAKEHOLDER ENGAGEMENT © OECD 2018

Roadmap actions

The actions outlined in the above Roadmap take into account the assessment of the current situation, the future activities of SFP in amending the CompraNet system, and the framework for the implementation of e-procurement systems. The table of Roadmap Actions presented below outlines the time frame in which the Roadmap suggests implementation, a description of each initiative and a short title for easy reference. Note that actions are aligned with Subgroup titles. However, some of the recommendations suggested by multiple Subgroups may have been consolidated into one action. Some actions may have been amended or removed, depending on the recommendations of this report based on international best practice. Recommendations are listed chronologically according to each Subgroup's alignment and the proposed term of implementation.

Each action is assessed against four "dimensions", which consider the types of changes necessary to implement the action. The four dimensions are: "*Tech*" – Technology, "*Process*" – Processes, "*Legal*" – Legislation and Regulation, and "*Gov*" – Governance, Structure and People.

3. A MULTI-PHASE ROADMAP FOR UPGRADING COMPRANET FROM COMPLIANCE TO INTEGRATION | 79

Table 3.1. Roadmap actions

ID	Title	Recommendation	Subgroup alignment	Dimensions Tech	Dimensions Process	Dimensions Legal	Dimensions Gov	Timeframe
1	Consult stakeholders on their information needs	Consult stakeholder groups on their different information needs; these must be understood in order to design effective search and analysis tools, and to ensure databases are appropriately structured.	Information disclosure				◆	Short
2	Data management strategy	Develop a data management strategy for the e-procurement system, ensuring information is comprehensive, readily available, and can be used effectively by stakeholders.	Information disclosure	◆	◆		◆	Short
3	Open data standards	Implement open data practices to normalise public procurement data and enhance accountability mechanisms.	Information disclosure	◆	◆		◆	Medium
4	Naming conventions and referencing standards	Enforce the use of naming conventions and agreed referencing standards to benefit the quality and searchability of data in the system.	Information disclosure	◆	◆	◆	◆	Medium
5	Reduce open data fields	Reduce number of open data fields, to minimise the possibility for data entry to compromise searchability and standardisation.	Information disclosure	◆	◆			Long
6	User friendly interface	Design a user-friendly interface for data access and analysis, and provide proper training for its use. Aim to ensure that ease of use of the system is a key feature.	Information disclosure	◆	◆		◆	Long
7	Article 1 exceptions within the system	Enable mechanisms to allow contracting authorities to use the e-procurement system for so-called Article 1 exceptions.	Information disclosure	◆	◆	◆	◆	Long
8	Identify barriers to supplier participation	Set a work plan to identify, with suppliers, barriers to supplier participation within the CompraNet tool, with special focus on small and medium-sized enterprises (SMEs).	Interaction with suppliers	◆	◆	◆	◆	Short
9	Expand training to improve suppliers' knowledge of the system's processes and functionality	Undertake efforts to improve and expand system training for suppliers to improve knowledge of the system's processes and functionality	Interaction with suppliers	◆	◆		◆	Short
10	Expansion of supplier registry to include prequalification information	Expand the current registry of suppliers to include additional information, such as bank guarantees, insurance certificates, professional qualifications and other documentation requested of suppliers during each tender process.	Interaction with suppliers	◆			◆	Medium
11	Standardised tender documents for common goods and services	Communicate standardised documents within the system for the procurement of commonly used goods and services	Interaction with suppliers		◆		◆	Medium

3. A MULTI-PHASE ROADMAP FOR UPGRADING COMPRANET FROM COMPLIANCE TO INTEGRATION

ID	Title	Recommendation	Subgroup alignment	Dimensions				Timeframe
				Tech	Process	Legal	Gov	
12	Standardisation of electronic documentation format and requirements	Enable the standardisation and streamlining of documents for procurement practitioners across government, including contract terms, general specifications and reporting requirements.	Interaction with suppliers	♦	♦		♦	Long
13	Transition to best practice standard for the classification of goods, services and public works	Implement classification changes so that goods and services are classified under a best practice standard; ensure regime is effectively applied and used by procurement officials.	Interaction with suppliers	♦			♦	Long
14	Procurement practitioner capabilities	Develop training procedures to increase e-procurement capabilities of the Mexican federal procurement workforce.	Competition and capacity building		♦		♦	Short
15	Identify required legal reforms	Identify legal reforms required to address recommendations for the improvement and expansion of CompraNet.	Competition and capacity building			♦	♦	Short
16	Support services for system users	Provide users of the platform support to maximise the benefits of the system through training and guidance (supported by help desk services), including promoting use of help desk services to those not currently engaging with the service.	Competition and capacity building	♦	♦		♦	Short
17	Audit approach developed by Internal Control Bodies on minimising exceptions	Internal control bodies to ensure CompraNet is always used, except in the case of valid exceptions.	Competition and capacity building		♦		♦	Short
18	Promote an inclusive reform programme	Promote an inclusive, multifaceted programme of procurement reform (such as legal and policy settings, or the private-sector environment).	Competition and capacity building	♦	♦	♦	♦	Medium
19	Contract management module	Build contract management capability by establishing centralised tools, such as a contract-management module.	Competition and capacity building	♦	♦	♦	♦	Medium
20	Open tender exception document disclosure	Establish mechanisms to disclose all public information to support a contracting authority's request for an exception to an open tender process.	Competition and capacity building		♦		♦	Medium
21	Development of monitoring and control approach	Development of monitoring and control approach to verify that users are using the system correctly.	Efficiency and effectiveness		♦		♦	Short
22	Ensure overall adherence to legislation	An initiative to encourage the consistent, systematised and transparent adherence to procurement legislation, such as in the selection of procurement procedures and use of tender exemptions. SFP should include the updating of the current CompraNet guidelines to address changes made as a result of this review.	Efficiency and effectiveness		♦	♦	♦	Short
23	Targeted audit investigations	Design data standards to allow audit authorities to conduct targeted, as opposed to random, audit investigations	Efficiency and effectiveness	♦	♦		♦	Short

3. A MULTI-PHASE ROADMAP FOR UPGRADING COMPRANET FROM COMPLIANCE TO INTEGRATION

ID	Title	Recommendation	Subgroup alignment	Dimensions				Timeframe
				Tech	Process	Legal	Gov	
24	Savings measurement methodologies	Implement savings measurement methodologies in relation to the amount of time saved through increased efficiency and by the amount of public and private funds saved.	Efficiency and effectiveness	◆	◆		◆	Medium
25	E-Signature enablement	Apply electronic signature functionality so contracts can be entered into the system in open-data format, removing the need for the scanned PDF format.	Efficiency and effectiveness	◆	◆	◆	◆	Medium
26	Integration with e-government systems	Promote integration of the system with other e-government technologies, such as public finance management, budgeting and service delivery systems, leading to better utilisation of public resources through better information transmission, automation, and increased accountability.	Efficiency and effectiveness	◆	◆	◆	◆	Medium
27	End-to-end system coverage of procurement cycle	Benefit from opportunities to increase efficiency through the expansion of the e-procurement system to cover the whole public procurement cycle, including ordering and invoicing.	Efficiency and effectiveness	◆	◆	◆	◆	Long
28	Promotion of whistle-blowing	Set up mechanisms to facilitate acts of whistle-blowing.	Prosecution of complaints	◆			◆	Short
29	Complaint mechanisms	Develop adequate feedback channels and complaint mechanisms, including specific instructions for filling complaints related to public procurement on the SFP website. Provide specific options or drop-downs in relation to public procurement and eliminate requirements for users to indicate which federal law they wish to complain under	Prosecution of complaints	◆	◆	◆	◆	Medium
30	Ensure adherence to document upload processes	Ensure adherence to document upload processes by increasing user capability and incentivising compliance	Integrity and trust in the tool	◆	◆		◆	Short
31	Complete and reliable data	Implement system changes to promote reliability of data within the system. Such changes can include adding checkpoints and requiring the submission of complete and unchangeable information.	Integrity and trust in the tool	◆	◆	◆	◆	Short
32	Classification of tender information	Develop an agreement on classifying tender information as publicly available or only available to control entities.	Integrity and trust in the tool	◆	◆		◆	Medium
33	Enable block-chain tracking of decisions and documentation	Design mechanisms to allow full traceability of decisions and documentation through public procurement processes.	Integrity and trust in the tool	◆	◆	◆	◆	Medium
34	Tender evaluation module	Develop an evaluation module that can conduct automated evaluation against set criteria and weightings for appropriate tender processes (while also facilitating more subjective evaluation processes).	Integrity and trust in the tool	◆	◆		◆	Medium

Source: Produced by the OECD Secretariat.

References

Gartner (2015), *Magic Quadrant for Strategic Sourcing Application Suites*, https://www.gartner.com/doc/2977817?ref=SiteSearch&sthkw=magic%20quadrant%202015%20eSourcing&fnl=search&srcId=1-3478922254 (accessed on 14 September 2017). [6]

National Audit Office (2014), "Using alternatives to regulation to achieve policy objectives", http://www.nao.org.uk (accessed on 14 September 2017). [3]

OECD (2005), "Modernising Government - The Way Forward", http://www.oecd-ilibrary.org/docserver/download/4205131e.pdf?expires=1505400004&id=id&accname=ocid84004878&checksum=C264781D51914267049D3BFE9AB9598A (accessed on 14 September 2017). [4]

OECD (2014), "Government at a glance: Ex post evaluation of regulation", http://www.oecd-ilibrary.org/docserver/download/4215081ec040.pdf?expires=1505750256&id=id&accname=guest&checksum=35C761A82513332E76ECE50303721E86 (accessed on 18 September 2017). [5]

OECD (2017), "Development and implementation of a national e-procurement strategy for the Slovak Republic", http://oecdshare.oecd.org/gov/sites/govshare/psi/PProcurement/Slovakia%20EU%20Project%2020162017/Final%20Deliverables/slovakia-e-procurement-strategy.pdf (accessed on 18 September 2017). [1]

Procurement Harmonization Project of the Asian Development Bank, T. (2004), "Electronic Government Procurement Roadmap", http://siteresources.worldbank.org/INFORMATIONANDCOMMUNICATIONANDTECHNOLOGIES/Resources/eGPRoadMap.pdf (accessed on 14 September 2017). [2]

Annex A. System 'Vision'

The development of a shared vision statement for Mexico's e-Procurement system (CompraNet) was proposed by members of the Subgroups. The Subgroups led the initiative to develop a document that could serve as a guide for the future state of CompraNet, by declaring a list of strategic objectives for Mexico's federal e-Procurement system to achieve in the coming years. From its origin, the document was treated as a collaborative product that every Subgroup member could agree upon; this practice was in line with the spirit of collaboration that was a foundational principle of the Working Group. All Subgroups agreed on this initiative, and a first draft of the vision statement was prepared soon after. In total, five draft versions were developed from July to October 2017, and a final statement was presented for the Working Group's consideration during the sixth Plenary Meeting. The final vision statement received a unanimous vote; the document is included in Chapter 1 of this Review (see Box 1.6.).

The first draft document included a list of 50 desired strategic objectives for Mexico's e-Procurement system. The main objectives of this first draft were kept throughout all draft versions and the final vision statement, which related to an e-Procurement system that:

- can be used by all levels of government (federal, state and municipal)
- includes all procurement processes, regardless of the contract awarding method (direct award, restricted invitation, public tender or other extraordinary award methods, such as Article 1 exemptions).[1]

On 26 July, the OECD as Technical Secretariat of the Working Group took on the task of co-ordinating the development of the vision statement and managing the draft versions, to include comments from the Subgroups and Mexico's Ministry of Public Administration (SFP). On 23 August, a second version of the draft was shared with SFP, and comments were received from the Unit for Public Procurement Policy (UPCP) and the Unit of Open Government and International Co-operation Policies (UPAGCI). Suggestions from SFP's units were included in a third draft version and shared with Subgroups for a further review on 6 September. From 7-11 September, the Technical Secretariat received comments on the draft vision statement from Mexico's Institute for Competitiveness (*Instituto Mexicano para la Competitividad*, IMCO), the local chapter of Transparency International (*Transparencia Mexicana*), *México Evalúa*, and the Business Co-ordinator Council (*Consejo Coordinador Empresarial*). This combined effort between Subgroups and SFP resulted in the fourth draft of the vision statement, which was shared with SFP on 14 September. The fourth version included a condensed list of 12 strategic objectives for Mexico's e-Procurement system (reduced from the 50 originally proposed).

After SFP's review of the fourth draft version on 18 September, the Technical Secretariat shared a final draft version with the Subgroups and SFP on 2 October. Remarks from *México Evalúa* and SFP's UPAGCI were incorporated, and a fifth draft version was distributed to attendees before the sixth Plenary Meeting on 9 October. During the sixth Plenary Meeting, the Technical Secretariat presented the final draft version of the vision statement for the Working Group's consideration. After only one minor suggestion by the

Business Co-ordinator Council, the document obtained unanimous support, which resulted in a request to the Technical Secretariat to include the final version in the OECD Review of the Mexican e-Procurement system.

Table A A.1. Timetable for developing a vision statement for Mexico's e-Procurement System

Proposal for the development of a shared Vision Statement	
11-Jul	• The Technical Secretariat (TS) invites Subgroup Co-ordinators (SGCs) to develop a vision statement (VS), following a proposal by IMCO and *Transparencia Mexicana*.
First draft of the vision statement	
18-Jul	• *Transparencia Mexicana* shares the first draft version of the VS.
19-Jul	• *México Evalúa* shares its comments on the draft version with the SGCs. • SFP (Complaints) shares its comments on the draft version with the SGCs. • Business Co-ordinator Council shares its comments on the draft version with the SGCs.
23-Jul	• COFECE shares its comments on the draft version with the SGCs.
25-Jul	• IMCO shares its comments on the draft version to with SGCs.
TS' involvement with the co-ordination of the vision statement	
26-Jul	• TS receives a request from SFP to co-ordinate the VS document, as well as the drafting and reviewing process.
Second draft of the vision statement	
23-Aug	• TS shares the draft version with SFP for comments.
1-Sep	• SFP (UPAGCI) shares its comments on the draft version with the TS.
4-Sep	• SFP (UPCP) shares its comments on the draft version with the TS
6-Sep	• TS shares the draft version with SFP for comments
Third draft of the vision statement	
6-Sep	• TS shares the draft version with SGC for comments.
7-Sep	• IMCO shares its comments on the draft version with the TS.
11-Sep	• Business Co-ordinator Council shares its comments on the draft version with the TS. • *México Evalúa* shares its comments on the draft version with the TS. • *Transparencia Mexicana* shares its comments on the draft version with the TS.
Fourth draft of the shared vision statement	
14-Sep	• TS shares the draft version with SFP for comments.
18-Sep	• SFP shares its comments on the draft version with the TS.
Fifth draft of the Vision Statement	
02-Oct	• TS shares the draft version with SGC and SFP for comments.
04-Oct	• *México Evalúa* shares its comments on the draft version with the TS.
05-Oct	• SFP (UPAGCI) shares its comments on the draft version with the TS.
Final vision statement included in the OECD Review	
06-Oct	• TS shares the draft version with SGC for comments.
09-Oct	• TS presents the draft version document to be voted and approved by the Working Group during the sixth Plenary Meeting. The draft version document is approved unanimously, with comments presented by the Business Co-ordinator Council.
10-Oct	• Vision statement is included in the OECD Review of the Mexican e-Procurement System.

Note

[1] Contracts entered into between contracting authorities and other contracting authorities or state-owned entities (for example, universities), under what is known as an Article 1 exemption (*Article 1, fifth paragraph, LAASSP & Article 1, fourth paragraph, LOPSRM*), are not required (nor allowed) to be entered into CompraNet.

Annex B. Subgroup recommendations

As part of the collaborative work undertaken by the Working Group, from February to July 2017 each Subgroup developed a series of recommendations for the expansion and improvement of CompraNet. Recommendations were developed in four steps: information gathering, information analysis/diagnosis, recommendation development (using a standardised format agreed upon by all Subgroups), and recommendation aggregation by the Technical Secretariat. In total, 21 recommendations were considered for this Review.

Steps 1 and 2: Information gathering and diagnosis of the current state of CompraNet

During the first Plenary Meeting, held on 28 February 2017, the Working Group defined a working timetable that involved each Subgroup developing a diagnosis based on the evidence they collected on the current state of CompraNet. These diagnoses, which were then shared by every Subgroup during the third Plenary Meeting on 8 May 2017, were developed using different information sources, such as *ad hoc* surveys (applied to suppliers, procurement officials and CSOs), document reviews, personal interviews, institutional questionnaires and data analyses. Each Subgroup was free to choose the information-gathering methods that best suited its needs.

The main methods used by Subgroups for gathering information – as inputs for their diagnoses – were as follows:

- Document review of previous works on public procurement by Mexican and international organisations such as *Transparencia Mexicana*, *México Evalúa*, Mexico's National Institute on Statistics and Geography (INEGI), the World Bank, the European Commission, and the OECD.
- *Ad hoc* electronic surveys prepared for businesses (suppliers), public officials, CSOs and journalists. Each e-survey had its own response rate and number of valid answers considered for analysis: suppliers (50 responses), public officials (148 responses), and CSOs and journalists (5 responses each).
- A paper-based questionnaire addressed to different institutions (COFECE, the Superior Audit Body, and the Co-ordination Unit of Internal Control Bodies of the SFP) was included as part of the information-gathering efforts.

Electronic surveys were one of the most relevant sources of information, as they were designed to reach a broad audience of stakeholders, mainly suppliers and public officials. Some of the main insights obtained through these surveys are:

- *Suppliers:* i) SMEs are less likely than large businesses to be awarded a contract.[1] ii) SMEs find CompraNet system functions more difficult to use than large businesses.[2] iii) SMEs are offered considerably fewer opportunities for training and capacity building in the use of CompraNet than large businesses.[3] iv) Bid opportunities, award decisions and clarification meetings are considered by suppliers to be the categories where information in CompraNet is most useful, accessible and adequate. Complaints and audits are ranked last against these measures (see Table B.1). *v)* One-third of businesses argue they have been victims of corruption but have not filed formal complaints because of a lack of trust in investigating authorities or because they consider the complaints process to be inefficient for whistle-blowers.[4]

Table A B.1. Information quality ranking

Quality of information in CompraNet regarding information's sufficiency, accessibility, timely information, and usefulness

	Sufficiency	Accessibility	Timely information	Usefulness	**Average**
Call for bids (n=157)	3.75	3.79	3.62	3.85	**3.75**
Award (n=156)	3.68	3.64	3.56	3.79	**3.66**
Clarification meetings (n=156)	3.63	3.67	3.33	3.74	**3.59**
Proposals and market rates (n=142)	3.39	3.17	3.31	3.59	**3.36**
Direct award report (n=141)	3.24	3.19	3.11	3.83	**3.34**
Information of the programme or project for which the procurement process is carried out (n=144)	3.57	3.22	3.11	3.11	**3.25**
Normativity (n=126)	3.03	2.91	2.84	3.56	**3.08**
Standards, rules, procedures and authorisations required for recruitment (n=134)	3.09	3.03	2.74	3.14	**3.00**
Tutorials and training (n=117)	2.86	3	2.76	3.3	**2.98**
Contracts (n=127)	2.94	2.79	2.9	3.16	**2.94**
Dispute resolution (n=101)	2.67	2.81	2.77	3.2	**2.86**
Public Procurement Programme (information on awards and contracts to be awarded) (n=123)	3	2.54	2.72	3.15	**2.85**
Statistics on public procurement (n=107)	2.8	2.58	2.5	2.94	**2.70**
Modifying agreements to contracts (n=113)	2.73	2.52	2.52	3	**2.69**
Information on market research: prices, suppliers, inputs (n=126)	2.48	2.34	2.42	3.46	**2.67**
Contract management and execution (n=113)	2.61	2.69	2.41	2.87	**2.64**
Global report on contracting (award and execution of contracts) (n=110)	2.67	2.6	2.41	2.84	**2.63**
Procurement officers: integrity, experience, performance (n=134)	2.5	2.55	2.47	2.91	**2.60**
Observations and recommendations of the Superior Audit Body audits (n=95)	2.52	2.52	2.52	2.82	**2.59**
Observations and recommendations of the Internal Control bodies audits (n=99)	2.36	2.39	2.52	2.89	**2.54**
Complaints (n=92)	2.5	2.38	2.17	2.96	**2.50**

Note: Using an ascending scale (with values ranging from 1 to 5, where 1 is the lower value of the scale and 5 the maximum).
Source: OECD analysis on the database for the electronic survey to suppliers, Plural Working Group on Public Procurement.

- *Public officials: i)* The smaller the procurement unit, the more likely it is for procurement officials to consider electronic storage of procurement documents to be of the same legal standing as maintaining physical archives.[5] *ii)* Procurement officials use CompraNet for some steps of the procurement process more than others, i.e. request for bids are more commonly uploaded to the e-Procurement tool than bid evaluations;[6] *iii)* Large and medium procurement units have received considerably more training for the use of CompraNet than small procurement units.[7] *iv)* Smaller procurement units consider CompraNet to be less effective in reducing integrity risks on public procurement.[8]

Based on the results of these diagnoses, each Subgroup was asked to develop a list of recommendations for the expansion and improvement of CompraNet. Subgroup recommendations were expected to acknowledge the current state of CompraNet and address current areas of opportunity to advance Mexico's e-Procurement system.

Table A B.2. Information-gathering methods, by Subgroup

Subgroup	Subgroup co-ordinator (participants)	Information-gathering method and sources
Information disclosure	**México Evalúa** (Business Co-ordinator Council, CANACO, CMIC, COFECE, IMCO, INAI, *Transparencia Mexicana*)	**Document review** (Transparency metric in public works – MeTrOP; national survey on access to public information – ENAID/INEGI 2016; open data standards for procurement, *Transparencia Mexicana*; Alliance for Open Government "Public Procurement"); **e-Survey** (suppliers; procurement officials; CSOs; journalists); **paper-based questionnaire** (Superior Audit Body; COFECE; Internal Control Bodies-SFP)
Interaction with suppliers	**Business Co-ordinator Council, Confederation of Industrial Chambers** (CMIC, COFECE, COPARMEX, the Mexican Employers' Association, IMCO, INADEM, INAI)	**e-Survey** (suppliers); **Analysis** (Problem Tree Analysis methodology)
Competition and capacity building	**COFECE** (Business Co-ordinator Council)	**Interview** (to the General Director's Office for Business Intelligence at COFECE); **paper-based questionnaire** (COFECE)
Efficiency and effectiveness	**IMCO** (Cámara Nacional de la Industria de Transformación, Business Co-ordinator Council, CMIC, COFECE, INADEM, INAI)	**Document review** ("Best practice indicators for public procurement", Government of Scotland; "Compendium of good practices for integrity in public procurement", OECD; "End-to-end e-Procurement to modernise public administration", European Commission; "E-Procurement Golden Book of Good Practices", PwC; "E-Procurement: Opportunities and challenges", World Bank); **e-Survey** (suppliers)
Prosecution of complaints	**SFP** (Business Co-ordinator Council: CANACO, COPARMEX)	**e-Survey** (suppliers); **Analysis** (Review to the Comprehensive system of citizen complaints – SIDEC)
Integrity and trust in the tool	**Transparencia Mexicana** (Business Co-ordinator Council: CMIC, COFECE, CONCAMIN, IMCO, INADEM, INAI)	**Interview** (stakeholders); **analysis** (review on CompraNet information; review of current legislation regarding public procurement)

Step 3: Recommendation development

For the formal proposal of recommendations for the expansion and improvement of CompraNet, the Subgroups agreed on the use of a standard format. This format, the Single Format for Observations and Recommendations (SFOR) was first suggested by the Subgroup Interaction with Suppliers co-ordinated by CCE and CONCAMIN (Confederation of Industrial Chambers – *Confederación de Cámaras Industriales*). The idea to develop a SFOR document was presented to all Working Group members during the third Plenary Meeting on 8 May 2017. On 15 May, the Technical Secretariat shared a first draft for the SFOR template document with the SFP for comments and suggestions, and the Technical Secretariat then shared the revised template draft with Subgroups for comments on 26 May. The SFOR template was agreed upon by all Subgroups, and a clarification meeting between all group co-ordinators regarding the filling of the template document was held on 1 June. The main characteristics and components of the SFOR template document are as follows:

- includes a cost-benefit analysis as well as an analysis on legal changes that could result from the implementation of the proposed recommendations;
- provides a section for the description of the justification considered by each Subgroup for the development of recommendations.

Subgroups shared their final SFOR documents with the Technical Secretariat on 12 June. In total, 30 SFOR documents and 51 recommendations were received (Subgroups were free to develop a single SFOR document for each recommendation, or to group several in a single SFOR document).

The Technical Secretariat received the following recommendations from the Subgroups:

Table A B.3. Single Formats for Observations and Recommendations, by sub group

Sub groups	SFORs received	Recommendations received	Main issues addressed in the Sub group's SFORs
Information disclosure	13	13	Information disclosure; Documents supporting the complete procurement cycle
Interaction with suppliers	14	14	Information disclosure; Information availability for query
Competition and capacity building	1	8	Information disclosure; Information availability fo query
Efficiency and effectiveness	0	0	Analysis of process compliance in CompraNet
Prosecution of complaints	1	4	CompraNet's complaint module
Integrity and trust in the tool	1	12	Information registry; Information audits; Information disclosure

Step 4: Recommendation aggregation by the Technical Secretariat

Once the SFORs were shared with the Technical Secretariat, the OECD undertook an aggregation analysis on the 51 recommendations received. These recommendations varied, covering a wide range of issues that were later grouped into 21 general themes. The results of this frequency analysis identified two main topics that were prevalent throughout most of the SFORs:

- broad document and information disclosure for the complete procurement cycle (*end-to-end information*)
- development of, and strict general compliance with, open-data standards for the classification of goods and services (similar to the existing Single Classifier for Public Procurement, CUCOP).

Recommendations were aggregated by the Technical Secretariat and shared with the Working Group on 18 July 2017, during the fifth Plenary Meeting. From the Technical Secretariat's analysis, the original 51 recommendations were grouped into 21 categories. All recommendations expressed by Subgroups are considered within the Technical Secretariat's shortened version. The analysis also indicates the frequency with which each recommendation was mentioned within all SFORs received, as well as the total number of Subgroups that address each issue. Results of the aggregation analysis are illustrated below.

Table A B.4. Aggregated recommendations

General Recommendation	Frequency of sub groups that mention the recommendation in their SFORs	Frequency with which the recommendation is mentioned in SFORs
1. Information disclosure	4	17
2. Availability of information for query	3	9
3. Information registry/ data capture	3	8
4. Business Intelligence / Market Research	4	6
5. Tender notification	4	6
6. Complete transactional process	4	5
7. End-to-end documentation	3	5
8. Complaints module	2	5
9. Open data standards for the classification of goods and services (CUCOP)	3	4
10. Change log	3	4
11. Information download	3	4
12. Information audits	2	4
13. Supplier registry (RUPC)	2	3
14. Annual planning	2	3
15. Publication of tenders	2	2
16. Creation of new modules	1	2
17. System interconnection	1	2
18. Clarification meetings	1	1
19. Subcontracts and right of collection assignments	1	1
20. Contract execution	1	1
21. Favourable opinion of the Treasury, social services and bank guarantees	1	1

Table A B.5. Timetable for developing Subgroup recommendations on CompraNet

Setting information gathering methods and developing diagnoses on CompraNet	
28 February	During the 1st Plenary Meeting sub groups are assigned the task to develop a diagnosis on the current state of CompraNet
March-April	Sub groups define their information gathering methods including e-Surveys, document reviews, interviews and paper-based questionnaires.
8 May	Sub groups share their diagnoses with the Working Group during the 3rd Plenary Meeting
Development and implementation of SFORs	
8 May	*Interaction with Suppliers* Sub groups take a proposal for the development of a SFOR to all Working Group members during the 3rd Plenary Meeting. The proposal was approved by the Working Group and the Technical Secretariat (TS) was assigned the task to co-ordinate and manage the development of a SFOR template document
15 May	TS shares a first draft version of the SFOR template document with SFP for comments
26 May	TS shares a second draft version of the SFOR template document with Sub groups for comments
1 June	TS holds a clarification meeting with all Sub group coordinators to address any doubts regarding the filling of the SFOR template document
12 June	Sub groups share their SFOR documents with the TS for their future aggregation and analysis
Aggregation analysis on recommendations	
13 June - 17 July	TS undergoes an aggregation analysis on recommendations shared by the Sub groups in their SFOR documents
18 July	TS shares the final aggregation analysis with the Working Group during the 5th Plenary Meeting

Notes

[1] Contract awards for businesses actively using CompraNet during the last five years, by size of business: micro (43% of micro businesses have not been awarded at least one contract during the last five years), small (44%), medium (25%), big business (6%).

[2] Ease of use for the different system functions included in CompraNet, by size of business: micro (29% of micro businesses consider CompraNet functionalities easy to use), small (44%), medium (50%), big business (88%).

[3] Training and capacity-building opportunities for the use of CompraNet, by size of business: SMEs (33% of SMEs have been offered training and capacity-building opportunities for the use of CompraNet), big business (75%).

[4] Reasons for not filling formal complaints using SIDEC (SFP's complaint system) against public officials in cases of corruption on public procurement processes: there was no case of corruption to complain about (69%), there was at least one case of corruption to complain about, but businesses do not trust the investigating authorities or consider the complaint process to be inefficient for whistle-blowers (31%).

[5] Legal validity of electronic archives vs. physical archives for procurement documentation: small procurement units (6.5% of procurement officials at small procurement units consider physical archives to have more legal validity than electronic archives), medium units (13%), large units (17%).

[6] Use of CompraNet for different steps of the procurement process: request for bids (95% of procurement officials say they use CompraNet for this step), opening of bid proposals (82%), clarification meetings (79%), bid evaluation (61%).

[7] Sufficient training for the use of CompraNet: small units (58% of procurement officials at small procurement units consider they have not received enough training for the use of CompraNet); medium and large units (46%).

[8] Based on your experience, has CompraNet had, or not had, effects on integrity risks on public procurement vs. face-to-face methods? By unit size: small units (42% of small procurement units consider CompraNet has had no positive effects on integrity risks compared to previous face-to-face methods), medium and large units (13%).

ORGANISATION FOR ECONOMIC CO-OPERATION AND DEVELOPMENT

The OECD is a unique forum where governments work together to address the economic, social and environmental challenges of globalisation. The OECD is also at the forefront of efforts to understand and to help governments respond to new developments and concerns, such as corporate governance, the information economy and the challenges of an ageing population. The Organisation provides a setting where governments can compare policy experiences, seek answers to common problems, identify good practice and work to co-ordinate domestic and international policies.

The OECD member countries are: Australia, Austria, Belgium, Canada, Chile, the Czech Republic, Denmark, Estonia, Finland, France, Germany, Greece, Hungary, Iceland, Ireland, Israel, Italy, Japan, Korea, Latvia, Luxembourg, Mexico, the Netherlands, New Zealand, Norway, Poland, Portugal, the Slovak Republic, Slovenia, Spain, Sweden, Switzerland, Turkey, the United Kingdom and the United States. The European Union takes part in the work of the OECD.

OECD Publishing disseminates widely the results of the Organisation's statistics gathering and research on economic, social and environmental issues, as well as the conventions, guidelines and standards agreed by its members.

www.ingramcontent.com/pod-product-compliance
Lightning Source LLC
Chambersburg PA
CBHW082353220526
45470CB00008B/2730